Improving Schools
Through
COMMUNITY
ENGAGEMENT

Improving Schools
Through
COMMUNITY
ENGAGEMENT
A Practical Guide for Educators

Kathy Gardner Chadwick

CORWIN PRESS
A Sage Publications Company
Thousand Oaks, California

For information:

Corwin Press
A Sage Publications Company
2455 Teller Road
Thousand Oaks, California 91320
www.corwinpress.com

Sage Publications Ltd.
6 Bonhill Street
London EC2A 4PU
United Kingdom

Sage Publications India Pvt. Ltd.
B-42, Panchsheel Enclave
Post Box 4109
New Delhi 110 017 India

Printed in the United States of America

Library of Congress Cataloging-in-Publication Data

Chadwick, Kathy Gardner.
Improving schools through community engagement: A practical guide for educators / Kathy Gardner Chadwick.
    p. cm.
Includes bibliographical references and index.
ISBN 0-7619-3820-6 (cloth) —ISBN 0-7619-3821-4 (pbk.)
    1. Community and school—United States—Handbooks, manuals, etc.
2. Community education—United States—Handbooks, manuals, etc.
3. School improvement programs—United States—Handbooks, manuals, etc.
I. Title.
LC221.C53 2004
371.19—dc21   2003012504

This book is printed on acid-free paper.

04   05   06   10   9   8   7   6   5   4   3   2

Acquisitions Editor:	Rachel Livsey
Editorial Assistant:	Phyllis Cappello
Production Editor:	Diane S. Foster
Copy Editor:	Sally M. Scott
Typesetter:	C&M Digitals (P) Ltd.
Proofreader:	Doris Hus
Indexer:	Molly Hall
Cover Designer:	Michael Dubowe
Graphic Designer:	Lisa Miller

Contents

Preface

At the beginning of a new millennium, the challenges faced by America's public schools are overwhelming at best. Public school teachers serve a student population with increasingly diverse needs. In any given classroom, you may find special education students; gifted students; students who speak very limited, if any, English; students of average ability; and students whose circumstances at home make it very difficult for them to learn. The impact of societal challenges like poverty, homelessness, teen pregnancy, violence, and drug abuse can be seen every day in our classrooms.

At the same time, public schools are facing the mandate for greater accountability. Test scores are routinely used to compare school districts, and the debate over high-stakes testing rages on. The Bush administration's "No Child Left Behind" initiative calls for higher standards to be applied to all students, with annual testing in reading and mathematics to document results. Sixty-seven percent of the Americans sampled in the 34th Annual Phi Delta Kappa/Gallup Poll (Rose &Gallup, 2002) favor the use of annual testing to track student progress, and 68% support the use of a nationally standardized test.

Clearly, the demands on public schools have increased. Unfortunately, the resources available to public schools have not been able to keep pace with these increased demands. Politicians face more pressure from voters to lower their taxes. State funding formulas become more complex, and the disparities that result often shortchange the districts in greatest need. More school districts are finding it necessary to go to the voters with additional bond and levy referenda for building, renovation, and operating funds. Expenses for social and health services, transportation, and technology continue to increase, leaving fewer resources for regular classroom instruction.

A predicted teacher shortage places even more pressure on the resources available for regular classroom instruction. Demographic analysis indicates that, as a group, American teachers are aging. Currently, two-thirds of the approximately 2.8 million public school teachers in the United States are 40 years old or older (Ward, 2000). Retirements, combined with a high rate of attrition among teachers, will result in a projected national demand of 2 to 2.5 million teachers by the year 2013. American colleges and universities generate slightly more than 100,000 bachelor's degree graduates in education annually. The supply of new teachers is unable to keep pace with demand, for a number of reasons. Low salaries, the challenging nature of teaching, and the lack of opportunity for career advancement discourage many young people from considering a career in education. Current certification requirements make it difficult for older adults to make a mid-career move into teaching.

As if the financial and human resource pressures on public schools were not enough, most schools have experienced diminished parental and community involvement in recent years. Work by Robert Putnam (2000) and others has documented the fact that Americans are less engaged with their public institutions than they were 50 years ago. This phenomenon is due to a number of factors, which include urban sprawl, pressures of time and money, the popularity of electronic entertainment, and the birth of post–World War II generations who lack the civic-mindedness of their elders (Putnam, 2000).

Could this disengaged public become a driving force in creating a brighter future for public schools? Suspend judgment for a moment and consider the possibilities. If the public were truly to become a partner with public schools in educating our children, we would ultimately see an improvement in student achievement. A recent review of the education literature confirms that the involvement of family and community members has a significant impact on student achievement (Henderson & Mapp, 2002). More involved parents and community members mean more adults working together to educate children both within and outside the classroom. An engaged public means more people working together to find the best approaches to the need for adequate funding and school accountability.

But where are there any signs of hope? A 2002 poll, conducted by Public Education Network and Education Week, revealed that Americans rank education second only to the economy and jobs in terms of national priority (Puriefoy & Edwards, 2002). This poll also found that Americans see public schools as a critical community resource. They believe that quality schools help build stronger families, improve local economies, and reduce crime rates. School quality also influences where Americans choose to live, and education plays a major role in determining their choices in the voting booth. Education is a top-of-mind issue for most Americans.

CAN THIS BOOK BE HELPFUL TO ME?

The challenge to educators is leveraging this public interest in education to bring about citizen action in support of schools. What do we mean by "community engagement" and what strategies are available to make it happen? The value of community engagement has been well established, but resources that address the "how to" questions have unfortunately been more limited in number.

This book addresses that gap by providing a basic framework that can be used in designing and implementing initiatives to more effectively engage the community. K–12 school administrators, school board members, and teachers are the primary audience for this book, but community leaders and citizens who are interested in improving student achievement through community engagement will also find the book to be useful.

Each chapter focuses on a key aspect of the community engagement process. In Chapter One, the reader is introduced to the concept of community engagement, along with evidence supporting the relationship between an engaged community and improved student achievement. Chapter Two addresses the creation of a planning team for the community engagement process, along with the selection of an appropriate issue to initiate the engagement process. Chapter Three provides guidance on identifying constituent groups within the community, while Chapter Four describes the techniques that can be used to better understand the expectations and perceptions of these different constituent groups. This insight is used in Chapter Five to design strategies that will be most effective in motivating constituents to act in support of improving student achievement. As examples, action in support of schools might include greater parent involvement in a child's education, more school/community partnerships, more volunteer support, or increased efforts to ensure that schools are adequately funded. Sustaining the ongoing process of community engagement is the focus of Chapter Six, with special emphasis on the training needed to create an engaged citizenry.

The following summary links each chapter of the book with key questions that readers might ask about the community engagement process:

Chapter 1: What is community engagement? Why is an engaged community important to student achievement?

Chapter 2: What types of issues might be addressed using a process of community engagement?

Chapter 3: Who should be included in the community engagement process?

Chapter 4: What techniques are available to help educators understand constituent perspectives and expectations?

Chapter 5: What strategies are effective in calling constituents to action?

Chapter 6: What kind of training can help educators and their constituents to be more effective in creating an engaged community?

With support from an engaged community, schools can do even more to help each student to achieve his or her full potential. The framework provided in this book will guide educators through each step of the community engagement process.

ACKNOWLEDGMENTS

This book has been shaped by the influence of many contributors. The initial idea for the book came from my work with K–12 educators through a leadership development program funded by the Bush Foundation. Discussions with devoted educators over a period of four years led me to pursue community engagement as a logical solution to myriad challenges faced by today's educators. More recently, contact with educators through a community development program funded by the Blandin Foundation has allowed me to further refine a "user-friendly" approach to community engagement.

I am also fortunate to have had the opportunity to learn from others who have had extensive experience with community engagement strategies. Jeffrey Kimpton, the former director of public engagement at the Annenberg Institute for School Reform, was very generous with his time, as was Jon Considine, formerly of the Collaborative Communications Group in Washington, DC. Both were involved in the Annenberg Institute's publication of *Reasons for Hope, Voices for Change* (1998), which inspired me with its stories of successful public, or community, engagement initiatives. Also, David Moore of the Harwood Institute was very helpful in sharing results from their "Reconnecting Communities and Schools" initiative.

Closer to home, I have benefited from the encouragement given by my colleagues who teach economics and management studies at St. Olaf College. Our administrative assistant, Pat Hall, can solve any word processing problem that comes her way. Student assistants Holly Malcomson and Jennifer Serafin also contributed their time to the final stages of text preparation.

And last, but certainly not least, I am grateful to my family and friends who were patient and supportive throughout this entire process. They listened when I needed to talk, and they gave me time when I needed to write. My daughter, Claire, and my son, Jim, deserve a special thanks for sharing their mom with "the book."

The contributions of the following reviewers are gratefully acknowledged:

Robert D. Ramsey, Ed.D.
Freelance Education Writer
Minneapolis, MN

Steve Hutton, Ed.D.
Highly Skilled Educator
On loan to the Kentucky Department of Education
Villa Hills, KY

Patricia B. Schwartz, Ed.D.
Principal
Thomas Jefferson Middle School
Teaneck, NJ

Karen H. Kleinz
Associate Director
National School Public Relations Association
Rockville, MD

William G. O'Callaghan, Jr.
William G. O'Callaghan & Associates
Lakewood, OH

Dr. Dave Mathews
President & CEO
Kettering Foundation
Dayton, OH

Heather Voke
Visiting Researcher and Lecturer
Georgetown University
Washington, D.C.

About the Author

 **Kathy Gardner Chadwick, Ph.D.** in marketing from Northwestern University, is the Husby-Johnson Chair of Business and Economics at St. Olaf College in Northfield, Minnesota. Prior to joining the faculty at St. Olaf, Kathy taught marketing at the University of Minnesota and worked as a marketing research analyst at 3M Company in St. Paul, Minnesota. For the past 20 years, she has served as a marketing consultant to a wide variety of organizations in both the private and the not-for-profit sectors. Her interest in community engagement stems from her background in marketing and her passion for education, combined with her opportunity to serve as a faculty member in a leadership development program for Minnesota educators, funded by the Bush Foundation. Conversations with K–12 educators over a period of several years convinced her that community engagement can address many of the challenges facing today's educators as they work to help students achieve at a higher level. Believing that "actions speak louder than words," she has been actively involved in her community's public schools, serving as cochair of the local elementary school site council, volunteering for district-level task forces, and regularly attending school conferences. She lives in Bloomington, Minnesota, with her two teenaged children, Claire and Jim.

1

How Does an Engaged Community Improve Student Achievement?

There seems to be widespread consensus that the public has been abdicating its responsibility for public education over the past four or five decades. More recently, Benjamin Barber (1992) described a modern America where rights and obligations have gradually become uncoupled. Continues Barber,

It [America] is a place where individuals regard themselves almost exclusively as private persons with responsibilities only to family and job, yet possessing endless rights against a distant and alien state in relationship to which they think of themselves, at best, as watchdogs and clients and, at worst, as adversaries and victims. There is apparently nothing government can do right, and nothing markets can do wrong. (p. 232)

1

When Americans see something in their government that they do not like, their first inclination is to blame their elected representatives. But in a democracy, these elected representatives should bear only part of the responsibility. According to David Mathews (1994), "The responsibilities for defining the public interest, describing the purposes and direction consistent with those interests, creating common ground for action, generating political will, and creating citizens are undelegable. . . . We can elect our representatives, but not our purposes" (p. 11).

Public schools are among the many institutions that have felt the effects of abandoned public responsibility. A recent report by Public Agenda (Farkas, Foley, & Duffett, 2001) on the lack of public involvement in education concludes that "the issue seems to be less a problem of opportunity and more a problem of complacency" (p. 15). In their survey of the general public, two-thirds of respondents said they were comfortable with leaving school policies for educators to decide. Only when people think their schools are performing poorly do they express a greater willingness to become involved. An alternative explanation is offered by David Mathews (1996), who served as the secretary of Health, Education, and Welfare in the Ford administration. He proposes that many Americans no longer believe the public schools are *their* schools. Reviewing more than 10 years of research by the Kettering Foundation, Mathews concludes that many recent school reform initiatives (i.e., increased financial control by state governments and professionally established standards) have actually served to further distance the public from its schools. Although many educators focus on ways to improve student performance or to enhance communication with public stakeholders, few are addressing what may be undermining improvement in performance or communication. Mathews writes, "Citizens complain that educators are preoccupied with their own agendas and don't address public concerns about discipline and teaching the basics. This lack of responsiveness is part of what convinces people that the public schools aren't really theirs" (pp. 3–4). Americans don't see the public schools as agents for creating a better society; instead, they focus on how public schools will meet the needs of *their own* children. Mathews posits that community development must precede school reform. In other words, there must be a *public* before there can be *public schools.* If we focus on public life in our communities and encourage more responsible citizenship, then we have laid the necessary foundation for true school reform.

Harvard professor Robert Putnam (2000) echoes this concern for a declining sense of community in America. He notes a serious decline in social capital, which refers to "connections among individuals—social networks and the norms of reciprocity and trustworthiness that arise from them" (p. 19). Putnam bases his conclusion on trends that include declining political participation, lower levels of participation in organized religion, and fewer memberships in clubs and community associations. Building on Putnam's work, the Social Capital Community Benchmark Survey (Saguaro Seminar on Civic Engagement in America, 2001), completed in late 2000, compared 40 communities across dimensions of social capital. The survey addressed two dimensions of "social trust" (trust of others), two measures of political participation, two measures of civic leadership and association involvement, a measure of giving and volunteering, a measure of faith-based engagement, a measure of informal social ties, a measure of the diversity of friendships, and a measure of the distribution of civic engagement across social classes within the community. Survey results, along with a more detailed description of methodology, can be found at: *http://www.cfsv.org/communitysurvey/results_matrix.html.*

It would certainly appear that social capital is a multifaceted concept and that the United States has seen a recent decline in most of the indicators used to describe social capital. But why have we seen this decline over the past several decades? Using a vast amount of data collected over the past 25 years, Putnam (2000) has concluded that four main factors are responsible for the decline in social capital:

- Pressures of time and money, especially in dual career families, that work against community involvement

- Suburbanization, commuting, and sprawl
- Privatization of leisure time through electronic entertainment, such as the television
- The replacement of the long civic-minded generation (born between 1901 and 1924) by their less involved children and grandchildren

An educator may find this decline in social capital of general interest but could be tempted to ask, "How does this affect my school?" In his book, Putnam reports a correlation between social capital and student performance. Social capital is highly correlated with student scores on standardized tests and the rate at which students stay in school. He offers some possible explanations for why social capital has such a marked effect on educational outcomes. First, in communities where there are higher levels of social capital, teachers report higher levels of parental support and lower levels of student misbehavior. There seems to be a sense of connectedness and accountability associated with social capital. Another reason why students may perform better in communities with high levels of social capital is that they watch less television. There is a negative correlation between the average amount of time that kids spend watching television and the average level of adult involvement in the community (Putnam, 2000). It appears that children are drawn into more productive uses of leisure time in communities where the levels of social capital and public involvement are higher.

Research over the past 30 years has verified that when families are involved with their children's education, children do better in school and the schools they attend are better (Henderson & Berla, 1994; Henderson & Mapp, 2002; U.S. Department of Education, 1994). Family involvement means children attend school more regularly, demonstrate more positive attitudes and behaviors, complete more homework, earn higher grades, receive higher scores on standardized tests, graduate from high school at higher rates, and are more likely to enroll in higher education. Henderson and Mapp (2002) recently completed a literature review of 51 studies that examined the impact of school, family, and community connections on student achievement. The research they reviewed confirms the value of family involvement in improving student achievement, but the evidence also points to the important role that communities play in the education process. Henderson and Mapp (2002) reported that community organizing resulted in "upgraded school facilities, improved school leadership and staffing, higher quality learning programs for students, new resources and programs to improve teaching and curriculum, and new funding for afterschool programs and family supports" (p. 57). They note that high levels of parent and community involvement are among the important factors that characterize high performing schools. Clearly, family and community involvement play a role in helping students achieve their full potential. For more detailed information regarding specific studies on the relationship between family/community involvement and student achievement, consult the Web site for the National Center for Family and Community Connections with Schools (*www.sedl.org/ connections*).

The fact remains, however, that social capital has seen a decline in recent decades. Americans appear to be less involved in civic activities and feel "less connected" to one another. They feel less committed to public institutions. Public schools have felt the impact of a less engaged public in the form of reduced parental involvement and declining community support for public education.

WHAT IS PUBLIC, OR COMMUNITY, ENGAGEMENT?

Certainly, the public bears some of the responsibility for their lack of engagement with public schools. But educators must also make an effort to reach out to their constituencies in order to encourage engagement. Currently, the public is characterized as disenfranchised at worst, complacent at best. The effort to reach out does not mean more public relations but a genuine attempt to hear what the public has to say by involving them in dialogue. The Annenberg Institute has defined "public engagement" as *"a purposeful effort, starting in either the school system or the community, to build a collaborative constituency for change and improvement in schools"* (Annenberg Institute, 1998, p. 16). The National School Boards Association defines "public engagement" as *"an ongoing, collaborative process during which the school district works with the public to build understanding, guidance, and active support for the education of the children in its community"* (Resnick, 2000, p. 1). (It should be noted that although earlier work makes use of the term "public engagement," "community engagement" is the term now preferred by educators to describe these efforts.) Both of these definitions incorporate what the Annenberg researchers identified as the five shared characteristics of public engagement initiatives (Annenberg Institute, 1998):

1. An inclusive and dialogue-driven process

2. A dedication to making meaningful and long-term improvement in schools

3. A commitment to creating dynamic, two-way partnerships

4. Sincere efforts to find common ground

5. An atmosphere of candor and mutual trust

To further understand what is meant by community engagement, it is perhaps useful to understand what community engagement is *not*. Mathews (1996) makes a clear distinction between an "engaged public" and a "persuaded populace" (p. 39). A "persuaded populace" is the desired result of traditional public relations efforts. As Mathews notes,

> public relations efforts can persuade people and gather support for good causes, but they can't create genuine publics. Publics are formed when people decide, among themselves, to live and act in certain ways. Making these decisions together gives their choices legitimacy and moral force.

Deborah Wadsworth, executive director of Public Agenda, stresses that community, or public, engagement is much more than informing the public or persuading them to believe as the experts do. According to Wadsworth (1997), "Public engagement presupposes a much more collaborative process in which individuals and groups think through issues together in a struggle to arrive at solutions they can all live with" (p. 750).

All definitions of community engagement seem to incorporate the concept of collaboration. But what is collaboration? How is it different from other strategies for working together? Arthur Himmelman (1994) sees strategies for working together on a continuum of complexity and commitment. "Networking," the most basic strategy, is defined by Himmelman as *exchanging information for mutual benefit*. "Coordinating" is defined as *exchanging information and altering activities for mutual benefit and to achieve a common purpose*. "Cooperating" is defined as *exchanging information, altering activities, and sharing resources for mutual benefit and a common purpose*. Finally, "collaborating" is defined as *exchanging information, altering activities, sharing resources, and enhancing the capacity of another for mutual benefit and to achieve a common purpose* (Himmelman, pp. 1–2). Each party in a collaborative effort is committed to helping its partners become better at what they do. Collaboration requires substantial time commitments and very high levels of trust, and it is characterized by extensive areas of common turf. Another term for community engagement might be Himmelman's notion of "collaborative empowerment," where empowerment is defined as *"the capacity to set priorities and control resources that are essential for increasing community self-determination"* (p. 3).

Regardless of the differences in terminology, it is clear that community engagement (or collaborative empowerment) involves much more than the traditional one-way communication flow from schools to the public. In *Reasons for Hope, Voices for Change*, the Annenberg (1998) research team describes how communication efforts differ from engagement efforts on a number of different dimensions.

COMMUNICATION	ENGAGEMENT
communicate to	deliberate with
public hearing	community conversation
talk to, tell	talk with, share
information out	information around
seeking to establish/ protect turf	seeking and finding common ground
authority	responsibility
influencing the like-minded	understanding those *not* like-minded
top down	bottom up
establishing a hierarchy for decision making	building a network of decision-making stakeholders
goals/strategic plan	values/vision
products	process
public relations	public engagement

It must be acknowledged that the process of community engagement carries some risk and requires educators to think about sharing decision-making power in nontraditional ways. An involved public can be threatening to those educators who are accustomed to unchallenged authority (Kimpton & Considine, 1999). It is hard work, requiring time, patience, and persistence. If educators do not understand the long-term benefits of community engagement, some may feel that they cannot afford the time commitment. Others may fear that people will be too critical of the schools and will not understand enough about the problems that educators face (Jennings, 1997). They may have had negative experiences with "the public," especially when encountering special interest groups. They may worry that the public will want to become involved in decisions that are best left in the hands of school faculty or staff. They may fear any loss in power. Still others may feel powerless themselves in the face of externally imposed reforms (Mathews, 1996).

Whatever the reasons for the discomfort, there are well-respected voices within the education community that argue for greater inclusion. Michael Fullan (2000) advises educators to "respect those you want to silence," (p. 159) because they may have important information and insight. "Move toward the danger in forming new alliances, instead of withdrawing and putting up barricades. . . . Boundaries of the school system have been permanently permeated" (p. 160). Seymour Sarason (1996) asks,

> Does it make sense to talk about schools as if they are part of a closed system that does not include groups and agencies outside that system? Why is it that when we use the phrase "school system" we think in terms of pupils, teachers, principals, school buildings, boards of education, superintendents, etc., and we automatically relegate other groups and agencies (e.g., parents, finance board, politicians, schools of education, state and federal departments of education) to an "outside" role? (p. 10)

He goes on to warn that those educators who overlook factors outside of the traditional "school system" will be less likely to achieve the desired consequences of their efforts. A former executive director of the American Association of School Administrators provides a more blunt version of the same message:

> We are going to be dead in the water if we don't find a better way of dealing with the public. For a whole variety of reasons, we have lost the public in many of our communities. . . . The public is going to end up supporting a lot of crazy ideas that are going to be disrespectful of the schools if we don't find more powerful ways of reconnecting the public with the schools. (Houston & Bryant, 1997, pp. 757–758)

How Does the Community Engagement Process Work?

There is no common blueprint for community engagement initiatives. Each school within each community will need to consider the specific characteristics of their situation to design a process that will work. Some of these considerations will include the complexity of the issues to be addressed, the level of trust that exists in the community, the extent of any organized opposition to or support of existing initiatives, the level of emotion associated with the issues to be addressed, the cost associated with these issues, and the time and budget available for the community engagement process itself. This may seem to be overwhelming at first, but a thorough situation analysis must precede the design of any community engagement strategy. Although adopting a "cookie-cutter" approach may seem desirable on the surface, a customized design is the best way to ensure successful community engagement.

Even though each school's plan for community engagement may be somewhat unique, there are some distinct phases that commonly characterize successful community engagement processes. They are represented in the framework that is shown in Figure 1.1, which will also be used throughout the remainder of this book.

Successful community engagement initiatives have a clear focus. Ultimately, improved student achievement is the goal of community engagement, but there are many routes to that final destination. For some school districts, a clearer sense of purpose and a strategic plan may be the necessary starting point. Other districts may need to start by addressing funding issues. Still others may need to begin by discussing the standards used to assess student achievement. Whatever the issue, community engagement initiatives need a focus. Chapter Two presents the issues that are most appropriately addressed by the community engagement process.

Because public schools serve numerous and diverse constituencies, care must be taken to include representatives from

Figure 1.1   A Framework for the Community Engagement Process

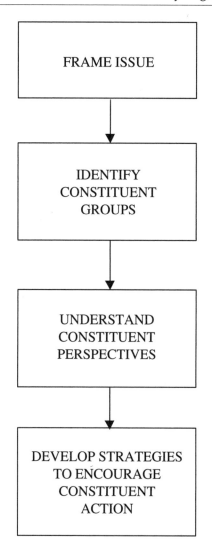

each of these constituencies in the community engagement process. Many school districts start by building a coalition of change agents representing these constituencies, who serve as a "planning team" for the process. Chapter Three addresses the task of identifying constituent groups.

Once constituent groups are identified, the next step is to develop an understanding of the varied perspectives that characterize these constituent groups. A variety of research and discussion techniques are available to facilitate sharing of different viewpoints. The idea here is not to persuade others but to understand them. Martin Marty (2001) makes an important distinction between "conversation" and "argument," which is worth noting at this point. Conversation is guided by the question and argument by the answer: "The movement in conversation is questioning itself—not confrontation, not debate, not an exam." Conversation requires respect for others, the willingness to listen, the acceptance of conflict, and the ability to change one's mind if the evidence supports a different position.

Thus, participants must avoid the temptation to rush to answers and action before an adequate foundation of trust and common understanding is in place. Mathews (1996) echoes this sentiment that publics must be reconstituted before they can be reconnected to the schools for the purpose of action. In other words, people must feel more connected to one another before they can begin the tasks of strategy development and implementation. Mathews notes that purity of intent is a critical factor in community engagement initiatives.

> Efforts to involve citizens, though well-intentioned and sincere, sometimes unwittingly treat the public as a means to ends that educators have in mind. . . . The public is not a means to the ends of educators, and people know it. They react adversely to many of the techniques used to involve them; though educators intend to empower, people feel manipulated. (p. 28)

If, after being asked for their opinions, the public believes that they have not been heard, the resulting damage is greater than if educators had proceeded without any public input. Chapter Four summarizes the techniques available for soliciting these opinions.

The fourth and final phase in the community engagement process involves strategies used to call constituents to action.

The desired action will differ depending on the circumstances; it may involve getting parents more involved in their child's education, building partnerships with community organizations to support schools, or encouraging voters to support a levy referendum. School districts that have experienced a successful community engagement process describe the energy that builds along the way (O'Callaghan, Jr., 1999b). Quantum theory can be used to characterize community engagement because the concept of critical mass is so important. The energy begins with a small group of people and spreads to a much larger group over time. Once the entire system is engaged, the possibilities for action are limitless. Chapter Five presents an array of strategies used by public schools to encourage constituent involvement and action. (The final chapter, Chapter Six, is not part of the framework for community engagement but will summarize the previous four chapters that do discuss this framework.)

How Does "Community Engagement" Help Schools?

This is truly the "bottom line" for educators. We know that community engagement is a *long-term* process designed to build commitment to and involvement in schools. The process will differ, depending on the unique characteristics of each school or district wanting to implement the process. We also know that there is risk in relinquishing some decision-making power to the public. Some educators have described efforts to engage the public as similar to dancing with a bear. You never know quite what to expect, and you dance until the bear decides it is time to quit. So why should school or district administrators be interested in community engagement?

First and foremost, a more engaged community results in improved teaching and learning. With support and understanding from the public, teachers feel less like scapegoats and more like professionals who are empowered to do the best possible job for *our* students. As members of the community, all of us have responsibility for educating our young people. "Teachers" are found outside of the classroom, in addition to those professionals within the classroom. The National School Boards Association has prepared a case study report documenting improved student achievement in response to public, or community, engagement initiatives in 15 different school districts (Saks, 2000). Educational research over the past 30 years has provided support for the claim that family and community involvement in schools has a positive impact on student achievement (Henderson & Berla, 1994; Henderson & Mapp, 2002; U.S. Department of Education, 1994;). Chapter Two will provide more detailed examples of successful community engagement initiatives along with documentation of results. Keep in mind, however, that it is somewhat naïve to expect that community engagement initiatives will guarantee significant measurable improvement in student achievement in one or two years. More likely is the scenario in which process outcomes (i.e., more dialogue, greater trust) will be evident in the short run, with improvements in student achievement coming over the course of several years.

So what kinds of process outcomes might educators expect as a result of a community engagement initiative? Certainly, greater levels of community trust in schools can be expected as one outcome. Also, school districts benefit from broader and deeper parent/community involvement in the schools when the public is engaged. This can be seen in more support for student learning at home, better attendance at school conferences and open houses, and more volunteers for all aspects of a school's functioning.

Time is not the only way in which the public indicates its support of schools. In recent years, changes in school funding formulas and continuing budget squeezes have sent districts asking for more money from voters. Across the country, community engagement initiatives have been instrumental in gaining voter support and increasing the financial resources available to schools, as we will see in Chapter Two. And, in some states, community engagement efforts have been the catalyst for the development of new policy and legislation to improve schools. For example, the Massachusetts Business Alliance for Education (MBAE), a group of state business leaders, helped the state legislature to draft and ultimately pass the Education Reform Act of 1993 (Annenberg Institute, 1998). On a more local level, the public schools in Aurora, Colorado, used a community engagement strategy to bring suggestions for policy changes to the Board of Education. A 50-person task force, composed of school and community members, studied the district's graduation standards and made recommendations to the board that were ultimately adopted.

Clearly, the outcomes from successful community engagement efforts are varied. This is due, at least in part, to the different purposes that community engagement efforts are designed to address. All have improved student achievement as their ultimate goal but may address different factors that influence achievement, such as greater parent and community involvement, increased funding, or standards development and implementation. Each of these is a legitimate focus for community engagement activity. The next chapter provides guidance on how to frame the issue for a community engagement initiative. Examples of successful initiatives are presented, along with the issues addressed and the results generated, where available. Key characteristics of successful community engagement initiatives will also be highlighted.

DISCUSSION QUESTIONS FOR CHAPTER 1

1. Given the definition of community engagement presented in this chapter, how would we evaluate our school's/ district's efforts to engage the public? What are the strengths and weaknesses of our current approach? Do these efforts fall more into the category of public relations or community engagement?

2. For our community, how would we describe the current level of public involvement in improving student achievement? Which groups of citizens are most involved? Least involved?

3. What is our vision of a community that is fully engaged in the improvement of student achievement? How does this compare with our current situation?

4. How might time and financial resources be made available for future community engagement efforts?

Framing the Issue
for the Community
Engagement Process

Careful planning is critical to the success of any community engagement initiative. Those who initiate the community engagement process need to be clear about the time and budget available for this work, and they must understand how public schools are currently perceived within the community. This provides important contextual information that will determine the design of the process. Planners also need to frame the issue that will serve as the focus for community engagement efforts. These issues should have significant impact on improving student achievement and, if possible, should naturally engage the energies and passions of the community. This chapter provides an overview of the issues that are most appropriately addressed through a process of community engagement. Before moving to a discussion of issues, however, let's discuss who is responsible for planning the community engagement initiative. Who will serve as a sponsor for this effort?

The Sponsorship Decision

Credibility, trust, and power considerations will be factors in determining who will sponsor the community engagement initiative. The sponsor is responsible for initiating the community engagement process and then performs oversight and reporting functions as the process continues. In some communities, the school board may be the logical choice for sponsorship, since board members serve as elected representatives of the public. School administrators may also assume the role of sponsor, but there is a danger that the public may perceive this to be a self-serving role for school officials.

If there is any controversy surrounding the community's schools, a neutral, "third-party" organization within the community may be a better choice for sponsoring the community engagement initiative. In some communities, a coalition of parents and other citizens have assumed the sponsorship role. The Prichard Committee for Academic Excellence is a group of citizens who rallied other citizens and the necessary resources to address the problem of educational mediocrity in Kentucky. Mothers on the Move, or "MOM," is a group of parents in the Bronx, New York, who formed an independent, nonprofit organization to improve their local schools. In other communities, a local education fund or community education foundation may perform the sponsorship role.

A local education fund is an independent community organization created to work with local school districts and the public to improve public schools and to promote student achievement (Public Education Network, 2001). Public Education Network is a national consortium of over 80 local education funds in 31 states and the District of Columbia.

Local colleges and universities could also serve as a neutral sponsor for a community engagement initiative, as could a community organization such as the League of Women Voters. Neutral parties can sometimes be more effective catalysts in bringing key constituencies together in dialogue. Because they are not affiliated with the school district, neutral parties may be in a better position to ask the "tough" questions and to keep the focus on the issue at hand. They may also have greater "staying power" because they are not subject to the turnover that characterizes many administrative and board positions within the school district. The Prichard Committee in Kentucky, for example, has been in existence for more than 20 years! Communities that are interested in pursuing a community engagement initiative to improve local schools have a number of possible candidates for sponsorship.

Each community will need to determine who possesses the necessary trust, credibility, and power to most effectively sponsor the community engagement effort.

CREATION OF THE PLANNING TEAM

The notion of assigning planning responsibilities to a nucleus of key individuals is nothing new. Epstein and colleagues (2002) suggest the use of "action teams" to encourage partnerships among schools, families, and the community. According to Epstein, a well-functioning action team has from 6 to 12 members, including at least two teachers, at least two parents, an administrator, community leaders, and students, if age appropriate. William O'Callaghan, Jr. (1999b) describes a "grapevine" effect that occurs as interest in an issue spreads from a smaller group of individuals to the community at large. And change expert John Kotter (1996) writes that creating a guiding coalition is a critical step in directing a change effort. He identifies four essential characteristics to consider when recruiting members for the guiding coalition:

1. *Position power*: Does the coalition include key players with authority?

2. *Expertise*: Are all perspectives on the issue represented?

3. *Credibility*: Does the group have members with good reputations in the community?

4. *Leadership*: Does the group possess the necessary leadership skills to drive change?

Once the guiding coalition (or planning team) has been identified, they will be responsible for designing a community engagement process that focuses on a clear and compelling issue, encourages dialogue with all constituencies represented in the community, and promotes action that results in improved student achievement.

Framing the issue is the subject of the remainder of this chapter, whereas the other planning responsibilities will be addressed in subsequent chapters.

FRAMING THE ISSUE

Issues that are most appropriately addressed by community engagement initiatives tend to be focused on broadly defined policy questions rather than the day-to-day issues of running a school. Most citizens have no interest in micromanaging public schools, but they would like a voice in defining student achievement and in creating standards to assess student achievement. Citizens would also like a voice in determining how schools are funded, since taxpayer dollars pay for public schools. And citizens have opinions about what would make it easier for them to become involved in public schools and the form that involvement might take. While all community engagement initiatives have as their ultimate goal improved student achievement, each community will have its own specific challenges that require attention. In some communities, school funding may be the primary current concern, while in other communities, the current focus may be academic standards. Figure 2.1 summarizes the issues most commonly addressed by community engagement initiatives.

This chapter will present examples of successful community engagement initiatives for each of the issues identified in Figure 2.1, together with a summary of the lessons learned from these initiatives. If available, data documenting the corresponding changes in the level of student achievement

Figure 2.1   Issues for Community Engagement

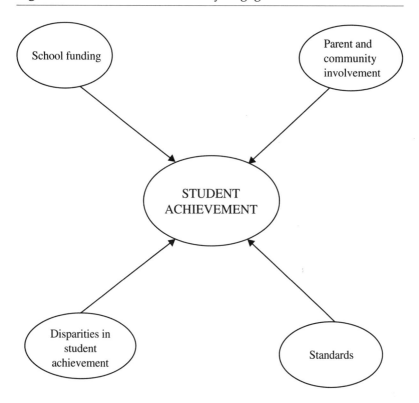

will be presented for each of these examples. It must be noted, however, that an engaged public is only one of many factors that ultimately affect student achievement. Average test scores, commonly used as measures of student achievement, reflect the combination of all influences on student performance (Meyer, 1996). Because average test scores reflect the cumulative impact of schooling, it is difficult to isolate the impact of a single, more recent initiative.

THE ISSUE OF FUNDING

In 1996, the Charlotte-Mecklenburg Education Foundation (CMEF), in Charlotte, North Carolina, found that voters lacked trust in the school district's information on school funding (Public Education Network, 2001). With the help of a steering committee and some additional research, CMEF published a "Community Guide to the School Budget" that was disseminated to the community through schools, local employers, and libraries. Local media promoted key themes from the guide, and the school board focused on redirecting funds as recommended in the guide. Because the school board perceived CMEF to be credible and unbiased, their recommendations were well received by board members.

As the result of community focus and reallocation of funds, Charlotte-Mecklenburg schools saw an increase in student achievement. From 1995 to 2001, the percentage of White 5th graders in Charlotte-Mecklenburg schools who were reading at grade level climbed from 76% to 96% (Charlotte-Mecklenburg Education Foundation, 2002). For Black students, the percentage reading at grade level in the 5th grade climbed from 35% to 76%. Continuing to look ahead, Charlotte-Mecklenburg schools have identified clear objectives for the year 2005 in five key areas: improving academic achievement (and reducing the racial gap), achieving a more equitable allocation of resources across schools, creating a safe and orderly school environment, strengthening community collaboration, and developing efficient and effective support operations (Charlotte-Mecklenburg Education Foundation, 2002).

In Houston, Texas, a community engagement initiative was launched after the business community rejected an attempt to raise taxes in 1992 (Saks, 2000). A key aspect of Houston's community engagement process is the PEER committee. A Peer Examination, Evaluation, and Review (PEER) committee is composed of experts from business and the community at large who address specific issues or problems in the Houston public schools. Since the inception of the community engagement process, Houston has passed a $678 million bond issue and test scores have improved. For example, 89 percent of fourth graders passed the reading portion of the Texas Assessment of Academic Skills in 1998, compared to 70 percent in 1994 (Saks, 2000).

In the state of New York, equity in school funding has been the issue. The Campaign for Fiscal Equity (CFE), a coalition of advocacy groups, school boards, and community organizations, brought a case to the New York Supreme Court in 1993, alleging that the state's system of school financing denied students in New York City their right to a sound basic education (CFE, 2000). The court of appeals upheld the right of CFE to challenge the state's education finance system. In January 2001, State Supreme Court Justice Leland DeGrasse ordered an overhaul of New York State's education finance system, requiring that the new system ensure sufficient resources to each school district so that all students have access to a sound basic education.

THE ISSUE OF PARENT
AND COMMUNITY INVOLVEMENT

In 1990, the Kentucky Education Reform Act (KERA) established standards for what all children should learn, along with an assessment system to measure their progress. KERA mandates that all Kentucky public schools must achieve proficiency in all subjects by 2014 (Henderson & Raimondo, 2002). And KERA gives parents representation on school councils so that they have more power to advocate for their children.

The Prichard Committee for Academic Excellence, a statewide citizen organization, is credited with being instrumental in the passage of KERA. Later, in 1997, they launched the Commonwealth Institute for Parent Leadership (CIPL), designed to make parents more powerful and effective advocates for improved education and higher achievement for all students (About CIPL Web site, para. 3). Each year, CIPL selects a diverse group of 200 parents from across the state of Kentucky to participate in the institute. The institute presents three, two-day sessions held in each of seven geographic regions of the state. Participant tuition, meals, and lodging are provided free of charge. Parents expand their understanding of their community's schools and the Kentucky standard-based education system. They also learn techniques for reaching other parents in their communities to encourage involvement in the schools. To keep the focus on results, the institute requires that participants agree to design and complete a project to improve student achievement in their communities.

In Texas, the Alliance Schools Initiative is working to increase student achievement in low-income areas by coordinating efforts of parents, teachers, and community leaders (Funkhouser, Gonzales, & Moles, 1997). Originating in 1992, the Alliance Schools Initiative is a partnership between the Texas Interfaith Education Fund and the Texas Education Agency. Franklin Roosevelt High School in Dallas is one of the schools implementing this approach. Through the Alliance Schools Initiative, a number of programs have been instituted to improve parent involvement at Roosevelt High School. A parent liaison was hired to make between 30 and 60 calls to parents daily. Arrangements were made to hand-deliver report cards to the home of every student receiving one or more failing grades. Training was offered to parents in how to support their children's learning at home and also on how to help themselves through computer literacy and language skills. Principals, teachers, and school staff were trained in how to form "core teams" that draw parents and community members into the decision-making process (Funkhouser et al., 1997). Each year, Roosevelt employees conduct a Neighborhood Walk for Success, making door-to-door visits to parents and community members in the area surrounding the school.

As a result, parents of Roosevelt students have become more involved in the school. Student achievement has improved as well, and Roosevelt is no longer on the Texas Education Agency's list of low-performing schools. Roosevelt students increased their scores on the Texas Assessment of Academic Skills from the 40th percentile to the 81st percentile in reading between the 1992–93 and 1995–96 school years. Over the same time period, Roosevelt mathematics scores went from the 16th percentile to the 70th percentile, and writing scores went from the 58th to the 80th percentile (Funkhouser et al., 1997).

A number of other communities have developed creative approaches to encourage parent and community involvement. In 1992, St. Louis Park, Minnesota, became the first community in the nation to fund a "Children First" initiative. The focus of "Children First" is to build "assets"—like family support, positive values, and structured use of time—so that young people do better in school and are less likely to engage in risky behaviors (Saks, 2000.) Romulus, Michigan, developed a districtwide "Parent Compact," specifying the roles and responsibilities of parents, teachers, and students. Both communities have seen increased student achievement in the form of higher test scores. In 1996, 66 percent of St. Louis Park 8th graders passed the reading portion of the Minnesota basic standards test. Seventy-six percent passed the math portion of the same test. In 1998, those percentages rose to 78 percent and 77 percent, respectively (Saks, 2000). Schools in Romulus, Michigan, recorded 49 percent of their 4th graders passing the state reading test in 1998, compared to only 17 percent in 1994 (Saks, 2000). Efforts are continuing to encourage parent and community involvement to drive future increases in student achievement.

THE ISSUE OF DISPARITIES IN STUDENT ACHIEVEMENT

In many communities, test scores reveal disparities in student achievement, depending on the student's race or socioeconomic status. Hattiesburg, Mississippi, participated in the National Conversations on Education and Race in the summer of 1999, jointly sponsored by Public Agenda and the Public Education Network. This discussion revealed a disconnect between parents and educators on a number of issues, including how to define and measure student success, the use of ability grouping, and the implementation of academic standards. Follow-up activities have addressed the clarification of standards, improvement of communication between school and home, and continued examination of the influence of race and socioeconomic status on student achievement (Public Education Network and Public Agenda, 2000).

In Kentucky, the Prichard Committee for Academic Excellence has teamed up with concerned residents of Jefferson County to create a Community Accountability Team (CAT) for the purpose of addressing the racial and socioeconomic achievement gap. The team decided to focus on middle schools in Jefferson County since they had the poorest record of performance progress. First, CAT set up a meeting with school administrators to review the district's achievement data (Henderson & Raimondo, 2002). Team members did, in fact, find disparities within Jefferson County public schools between White and Black students, between male and female students, and also with other districts in Kentucky. They were also surprised to find significant differences between schools in terms of teaching quality, instructional methods, and the use of student-grouping practices. As a result of their investigation, CAT released a report titled "Every Child Counts" at a public event in January 2001. The report offered three main recommendations, complete with action plans (Jefferson County Community Accountability Team, 2001):

1. Hold high expectations for students at all achievement levels.

2. Individualize instruction so that all students can reach their full potential.

3. Build strong partnerships with families and community groups for raising student achievement.

To diversify its membership among low-income constituents, CAT recently formed an Engaging the Community committee (Henderson & Raimondo, 2002). They plan on going door to door to talk about the "Every Child Counts" report and what can be done to reduce the achievement gap. Racial and socioeconomic disparities in student achievement continue to be the subject of extensive public discussion as Jefferson County public schools work toward solutions.

THE ISSUE OF STANDARDS

Some communities find themselves addressing the issue of standards as their starting point for the community engagement process. In Gwinnett County, Georgia, citizens expressed dissatisfaction with the district's emphasis on outcomes-based education. They wanted to know what students were learning in the classroom each day, and they asked for a clearer explanation of curriculum objectives. The school board and administration responded by involving the public in the process to determine the Academic Knowledge and Skills (AKS) that students need to succeed in the workplace and in post-secondary education (Saks, 2000). In Minnesota, state lawmakers repealed the controversial Profile of Learning during the 2003 legislative session. They voted to replace the "show what you can do" standards with more specific content-based ("show what you know") standards. As more states wrestle with the design and implementation of meaningful standards, it makes sense to engage the public in these discussions.

KEY LESSONS LEARNED IN THESE INITIATIVES

Regardless of the issue addressed, some key common elements can be found in all of the successful initiatives described in this chapter. *First and foremost, the ultimate focus for all of these initiatives was student achievement.* While each community framed the issue to address their most immediate and specific challenges (i.e., funding, standards, etc.), the direct link to student achievement was clearly articulated. When possible, these communities attempted to assess the impact of the engagement initiative on measures of student achievement.

In addition, *successful community engagement initiatives are based on a shared vision regarding the purpose of a public school education.* Communities that are successful in improving student achievement must first have some common understanding of what they want public schools to help students to accomplish, together with a set of standards to assess progress toward identified goals. As an example, the state of New York has wrestled with the definition of a "sound basic education" in its attempt to provide equitable funding for all public schools. Based on extensive public discussion, the court of appeals in New York ruled that "a sound basic education should consist of the skills students need to sustain competitive employment and function productively as civic participants capable of voting and serving on a jury" (Campaign for Fiscal Equity, Inc., 2000, p. 3).

Perspectives on Purpose from the Education Literature

There is little consensus, in theory or in practice, regarding the fundamental purpose of public schools. Even a cursory overview of the education literature reveals a diversity of views on the purpose of public schools. Some scholars focus on multiple purposes while others single out a primary purpose. Goodlad (1994) provides a comprehensive look at the purpose of public school in his twelve goals for American schools. They are as follows:

1. Mastery of basic skills or fundamental processes

2. Career education

3. Interpersonal relations

4. Autonomy

5. Citizenship

6. Creativity

7. Self-realization

8. Intellectual development

9. Enculturation

10. Self-concept

11. Emotional and physical well-being

12. Moral and ethical character

Sizer (1997) offers a more compact list of functions for public education, as follows:

1. Civic function

2. Economic function

3. Cultivation

4. Development of intellectual strength

Sizer's civic function would overlap with Goodlad's (1994) goal of citizenship and perhaps the development of moral and ethical character. The economic function addresses the vocational element of education and the autonomy that accompanies economic self-sufficiency. Cultivation is a broad term, referring to those efforts that welcome students into our culture. Development of intellectual strength closely parallels Goodlad's notion of intellectual development.

The theme of training for citizenship and civic responsibility also appears in the works of Barber (1992) and Glickman (1993). Barber writes, "Public education is necessarily about the education of public persons, of democratic citizens devoted to a common set of legal and political principles that work both to ameliorate and to transcend differences" (p. 146). He then credits democracy with creating the "ideals of pluralism, tolerance and the separation of private and public that have permitted American multiculturalism to function democratically rather than destructively" (p. 150).

Glickman (1993) goes even further to suggest one primary goal for American public schools: preparing students to become productive citizens of our democracy. Currently, Glickman argues, American schools lack a core guiding principle; instead, they pursue many diverse purposes. As a result, constituencies are always ready to criticize the public schools for not accomplishing *their* personal agendas. Schools are focused on subgoals like how to bolster graduation rates or how to improve our international rankings in math and science instead of focusing on a larger, single goal. The result is fragmentation and an inevitable sense of failure when any of these subgoals is not achieved. Glickman explains that

> the essential value of the public school in a democracy, from the beginning, was to ensure an educated citizenry capable of participating in discussions, debates, and decisions to further the wellness of the larger community and protect the individual right to "life, liberty and the pursuit of happiness." (pp. 8–9)

Improved test scores, higher graduation rates, or any other success on an isolated subgoal will not compensate for the failure to produce an educated and engaged citizenry. Cuban (2000) agrees that this is why "good" schools are so hard to get.

> It is not because of an absence in expertise or a lack of will. . . . They are hard to get because few have examined carefully, deliberately and openly different conceptions of 'goodness' and how each view is connected to the essentials of democratic life. (p. 168)

Additional Factors That Determine Initiative Success

A focus on student achievement and a common vision regarding the purpose of a public school education will go a long way toward building a successful community engagement process. Additional key factors that are instrumental in determining the success of a community engagement initiative will be addressed in the coming chapters. These include:

- Board and administrative support for the engagement process (Chapter 3)
- Balanced representation of constituents in all aspects of the process (Chapter 3)
- Engagement strategies that are designed with a clear understanding of the targeted constituent group(s) (Chapters 4 and 5)
- Training in the engagement process for internal and external constituents (Chapter 6)

DISCUSSION QUESTIONS FOR CHAPTER 2

1. Who is in the best position to sponsor the community engagement process in our community: the school/ district or a third-party organization?

   Consider:
   - The current level of trust in the community's public schools
   - The volatility of the political climate surrounding education
   - The budget and time available through the school or district
   - Credibility and power issues

2. Who are the best candidates in our community for membership on the planning team for the community engagement process? Does it make sense to create subcommittees to oversee specific aspects of the community engagement initiative?

3. What issue makes the most sense as the initial focus for the community engagement process? Is this an issue that
   - the community would find interesting and important to discuss?
   - is directly related to improving student achievement?
   - is appropriate for discussion at this time in our community?

4. Is there a shared understanding regarding the purpose of public schools in our community? Are these expectations realistic, given the resources available to public schools in our community?

Identifying Key Constituencies in Our Community

Selection of participants for a community engagement initiative is obviously a critically important decision. Success of the initiative will hinge on the quality of recruitment efforts. The simple answer to "who should be engaged?" is "just about everyone"! Identifying internal and external constituencies will be the focus of this chapter, with a discussion of techniques used to understand constituents presented in the following chapter.

INTERNAL CONSTITUENCIES

Before the community at large is drawn into the engagement process, the planning team must make sure that *internal* constituencies are "on board." These would include members of the school board, administrators, and teachers. All school employees should be given the opportunity to offer their input. Without the support of these "insiders," any subsequent community engagement efforts can be easily derailed. Students and their parents are the next group of constituents to be brought into the process, followed by the community at large.

The School Board

The school board is in a perfect position to play a key role in the community engagement process. School board members serve as elected representatives of the public, and they are more knowledgeable than the average citizen about the issues facing the community's educators. In a sense, the school board serves as a bridge between the public and its schools. School board members generally support community engagement initiatives, but perhaps with less enthusiasm than superintendents do. Public Agenda (Farkas, Foley, & Duffett, 2001) found that 56% of the school board members they surveyed agreed with the statement that "educators should be primarily responsible for deciding specific school policies. That's their job" (p. 27). This compares to 37% of superintendents and 39% of teachers who agreed with this statement.

The Public Agenda researchers also found that board members strongly believe that the public has a responsibility to speak up about the issues that concern them. Educators cannot be expected to be constantly soliciting public input, according to school board members. Yet more than 75% of board members also agreed that "schools need to do a far better job of listening to the concerns of community residents" (Farkas et al., 2001, p. 31). It may be that school board members are somewhat ambivalent about the value of community engagement because of what happens at typical school board meetings. These meetings tend to attract only the most vocal and partisan members of the community. Special interests and emotional rhetoric characterize these discussions, thus leaving many board members reluctant to provide any more opportunity for public input. Public Agenda (Farkas et al., 2001) concludes it is a sad irony that, even though board members consider these meetings to be unproductive because of the constant complaints by special interests, a majority of board members do rely on them to understand the views of the community overall.

If a proposed community engagement initiative is to be successful, the support of school board members is a critical prerequisite, at the very least. Ideally, school boards would provide a leadership role in the community engagement process. In South Carolina, for example, in their "Reconnecting Communities and Schools" initiative, the state school boards association took an active role in organizing "community conversations" in four different school districts (McDonnell & Weatherford, 1999). In order to garner support and encourage leadership, however, some board members may need to be educated about the benefits of community engagement and then reassured that a broad cross-section of public opinion will be represented in the community engagement process. School board support is absolutely necessary as one of the first steps in planning a successful community engagement initiative.

Administrators

For administrators, finding time in busy schedules to facilitate the community engagement process will be a definite challenge. Superintendents and building principals may feel that this is just one more demand on their time. As with school board members, some education may be necessary so that the value of community engagement is understood. The potential benefits of community engagement must be made clear: greater parent and community involvement that has a direct impact on teaching and learning. Along the way, communities with high levels of community engagement see greater levels of trust in schools, more support for new funding initiatives, and increased willingness to address the important policy issues that have an impact on student achievement. For those administrators seeking a "quick fix," community engagement will only prove to be frustrating and time consuming. Community engagement is a long-term strategy; results will not likely be immediate. But the benefits are significant. Community engagement can, over time, relieve so many of the administrators' day-to-day pressures of dealing with improving student achievement, funding shortfalls, and determining standards for measuring student performance. An engaged public can make an administrator's job much easier in the long run.

Organizers of the community engagement initiative need to be honest with administrators about the time, patience, and persistence that are required. There is some risk involved in asking the public what they think. They will tell you, and you may not like it. Accountability will be an issue. The public will expect to see that their input has played a role in decision making. The school district risks greater damage by asking people what they think and then doing nothing about it, than if educators make no attempt to engage the public at all. Also, established power hierarchies may be threatened by community engagement. By definition, it requires the sharing of power that perhaps once was controlled by a few individuals. Administrators will need to be assured that the recruitment of participants for a community engagement initiative will not be limited to the malcontents who are always sure to complain. It does not have to be just one more opportunity for critics to attack the schools. Instead, community engagement can be a powerful asset to the school administrator. A variety of approaches exist for community engagement, so the unique needs of each community can be taken into account when designing a strategy. Community engagement can help administrators to work more effectively with their communities in improving educational opportunities for all students.

Teachers

Teachers are the remaining key internal constituency to be brought "on board" prior to engaging the larger community. Clearly, they are the "front line" in terms of interaction with students and parents. As such, teachers are a critical conduit of information about schools to parents and the broader community. The public wants to hear more from teachers in the quest to improve schools. This is the good news.

Unfortunately, teachers have not been a significant force in community engagement efforts to date. A number of factors probably contribute to this lack of involvement. According to Public Agenda (Farkas et al., 2001), 70% of the teachers they surveyed indicated that they felt "left out of the loop" when it came to district-level decision making about schools. Adequate "face time" with administrators does not appear to be the problem; instead, teachers cite lack of responsiveness to their concerns. Add to this the fact that few teachers are familiar with the concept of community engagement. Teachers also feel consumed with the day-to-day challenges of teaching. Many teachers complain about unrealistic expectations and the failure of school districts to establish priorities for teaching. Trying to please everyone results in failure to satisfy anyone.

Even when teachers become familiar with community engagement, they are skeptical. Writing in *Phi Delta Kappan*, Rob Weil (1997), speaking on behalf of teachers, explains their reservations. First, teachers see diminished parental support in their classrooms every day. They question whether the expectations associated with community engagement are realistic. And second, they also see elevated criticism of public schools by countless interest groups, many with no knowledge or factual basis for their claims. Teachers wonder how community engagement will be any different. According to research by Public Agenda (Farkas et al., 2001), teachers view the role of citizens as being rather limited. Teachers view citizens primarily as voters, taxpayers, and cheerleaders, instead of seeing ordinary citizens as having the potential to actively engage in education. This study reports that teachers want the support of the local citizenry but are not interested in hearing their concerns or getting their feedback on school policies. If this is true, teachers' narrow view of the public's role in the educational process will need to be addressed before any meaningful community engagement efforts can occur.

Even if teachers were educated on the benefits of community engagement and were fully committed to the process, barriers would still remain. Time is a huge concern; teachers already feel pulled in too many different directions. Administrators at the building and district levels will need to demonstrate their commitment to the concept of community engagement by making teacher participation a top priority. This means something else will have to be sacrificed in order to provide teachers with the time to participate. A common complaint among teachers is that responsibilities are always added to the job of teaching, without any effort to reduce the level of pre-existing demands on a teacher's time. This results in frustration and cynicism among teachers. Union leaders will need to be consulted regarding the nature and extent of teacher involvement in community engagement initiatives. Teachers also need to believe that their perspectives will be heard and valued by administrators before they will actively participate in any community engagement initiative.

Students

If schools truly are an open system, the distinction between internal and external constituencies is hard to make. One cannot draw a clear boundary separating the schools from the "public"; the community is part of the school system. Regardless of their classification, it seems obvious that students would be a primary constituency to be included in any community engagement effort. As the consumers of the educational product, students have a unique perspective. While it may be difficult for students at the elementary school level to articulate their viewpoints in a discussion among adults, older students could easily be included. Thus it may come as a surprise that students have seen minimal involvement in most community engagement initiatives to date. The research reported in *Reasons for Hope, Voices for Change* (Annenberg Institute for School Reform, 1998) uncovered few efforts that involved students in community engagement initiatives. In those communities where students were involved, they provided significant energy and insight to the process. For their part, students benefit from a better understanding of the connection between school and community, which may generate greater student interest in service to that community. Students also feel a greater commitment to their home town as a result of the community engagement process. This may encourage them to continue living in that community as adults. Those planning the community engagement initiative must make sure to include students from diverse racial, socioeconomic, and faith backgrounds.

Parents of Current Students

Parents are a more reasonable constituency than most educators realize. One of the biggest mistakes that educators can make is to assume that the public is hostile—an adversary to be neutralized. Certainly parents can be expected to be advocates for their children. But parents have no interest in being involved in every discussion about education. According to the research by Public Agenda (Farkas et al., 2001), parents are quite willing to delegate many education decisions to "the professionals." "In general, they [parents] respect their [educators'] judgment, and few seem eager to wrest control or endlessly second-guess decisions that depend mainly on professional experience and judgment" (p. 29). Most would agree that community engagement is not appropriate for the *details* of policy responses, day-to-day operations, or legal and personnel issues. But parents do expect to be forewarned and consulted in times of fundamental change. They expect to have the opportunity to evaluate policy alternatives, especially in times of crisis or community divisiveness. And they expect their most serious concerns to be heard with respect.

ENGAGING THE COMMUNITY AT LARGE

Capacity Inventory as a Planning Framework

As the planners of the community engagement initiative gain support from board members, school employees, current students, and their parents, it is time to begin engaging the community at large. Kretzmann and McKnight (1993) have developed an asset-based model of community development that may be helpful to planners of the community engagement process. They believe that communities become stronger by leveraging the human assets found within a given community, rather than focusing on the needs and shortcomings of that community. Dwelling on the deficiencies often results in a fragmented approach driven by myriad real or perceived problems. Leadership skills and a sense of self-sufficiency do not develop when the focus is on needs and shortcomings within the community. Preservation of the status quo and a "survival" mentality tend to be the outcomes of a deficiency-based view of the community.

In contrast, an asset-based approach to community development builds on what is already working in the community. It encourages self-sufficiency and the development of leaders from within the community. Kretzmann and McKnight (1993) identify four categories of community assets to be considered in a capacity inventory for asset-based community development. These categories of community assets can serve as a checklist of the key constituencies to be included in any community engagement initiative. They are as follows:

- Not-for-profits (i.e., citizens' associations, churches, synagogues, and cultural organizations)
- Publicly funded institutions (i.e., hospitals, libraries, parks, law enforcement)
- Businesses
- Local residents

Not-For-Profits

One way to build diverse representation into the community engagement effort is to sample from a variety of not-for-profit organizations in the community. These might include:

- Arts organizations
- Charities such as the American Red Cross, United Way, etc.

- Political organizations
- Religious organizations—churches, synagogues, Bible study groups
- Senior citizens groups
- Service clubs—Lions, Rotary, Kiwanis, Knights of Columbus, etc.
- Social causes—Habitat for Humanity, food banks/food shelves, etc.
- Sports leagues

While certainly not exhaustive, this list illustrates the diversity of interests and perspectives found in a community's not-for-profit organizations. In most communities, it will not be practical to involve representatives from all of these organizations in any one single community engagement initiative. Thus those planning the community engagement initiative must consider the relative power possessed by each of these organizations regarding education issues. In addition, the organization's level of support for education would be worthy of consideration. Is this organization an advocate for local schools or more likely to be a critic? Community engagement efforts will want to leverage the support of advocates while making sure that critics are included as well. This will allow educators to hear the concerns of critics, thus beginning a two-way dialogue with the goal of finding common ground.

Publicly Funded Institutions

In addition to not-for-profits, public institutions play a major role in the life of any community. Public schools are included in this category, as are hospitals, libraries, parks, law enforcement, firefighters, and city government. One might also include county, state, and federal legislators in this category. Thus it is important that public institutions be represented in any community engagement initiative. As was the case with not-for-profits, these public institutions will not all be equally powerful with respect to education issues. If it is not feasible to include representation from all of these institutions in the community engagement initiative, it is advisable to make sure that the most powerful ones are at the table. Supporters should be balanced with critics as well. Those institutions who are initially among the school district's detractors can become powerful advocates as a result of the community engagement process. As an example, the firefighters in a rural Minnesota community had a history of strong opposition to additional funding for schools. This was a group with strong internal bonds, and they possessed considerable influence within the community at large. The local teachers and school administrators made a concerted effort to begin a dialogue with the firefighters, hearing their concerns and sharing the challenges facing local schools. As a result of this engagement process, the firefighters became outspoken advocates for public schools.

Sometimes, public institutions need to be gently reminded that quality schools are key to their organization's future success. Hospitals are facing a future shortage of health care professionals; why not partner with the local schools to attract students to the health care professions? A strong math and science curriculum in local K–12 public schools will better prepare students for the necessary training in the health care professions. Community colleges, vocational schools, and colleges and universities should also have a vested interest in the quality of K–12 education in their community. The future enrollment in these postsecondary institutions depends, at least in part, on whether high school graduates are adequately prepared for further education and training.

Businesses

In similar fashion, local businesses depend upon the quality of "output" from K–12 public schools in the community. Local high school graduates will constitute at least part of the future labor force for those businesses. Managers expect that future employees will possess certain skills, expressing frustration when they believe that the public schools are not adequately addressing these skills. So it makes sense for local businesses to have substantial representation in any community engagement effort initiated by the schools. Businesses have considerable power in most communities because of the money and other resources they control; they also can be quite vocal when they are unhappy with the public schools.

Certainly, businesses can be recruited on an individual basis for the purposes of community engagement. Depending on the size of the community, this could be a rather time-consuming effort. Another strategy would be to work through organizations that serve local businesses or have business leaders as their members. These organizations would include the local Chamber of Commerce, trade associations, and service clubs like Rotary, Kiwanis, and others. Recognize also that some of these business leaders may be parents of current students and that others will not. It would be desirable to have a balance of both in any representation of business leaders. This would be true for those representing not-for-profit organizations and public institutions as well.

Local Residents

The constituency of local residents includes taxpayers who are not represented in any of the other constituencies identified up to this point. They do not currently have children enrolled in public schools and are not affiliated with a not-for-profit, public institution, or business in the community. A large proportion of this group of citizens is likely to be retired, given current population trends. Certainly nonparents, and seniors in particular, could be expected to have different views regarding K–12 public education, and as such must be included in any community engagement initiative. But it would be wrong to assume that nonparents are less willing to accept responsibility for public schools. According to the study by Public Agenda (Farkas et al., 2001) cited earlier in this chapter, 62% of respondents agreed that *all* taxpayers have the responsibility to get involved in school issues, compared to only 37%

who thought it was solely the responsibility of parents with children currently enrolled in public school. And most citizens state they are willing to "put their money where their mouth is" and pay more in taxes to support public schools. Forty-eight percent of nonparents are willing to accept a higher tax bill, compared to 52% of parents who have children currently enrolled in school. The Public Agenda researchers found little evidence for alienation and anger toward public schools among those who are nonparents. Instead, detachment seems to more accurately characterize this segment of the population. This is important for educators to keep in mind as they reach out to nonparents.

The Media

Certainly the media cannot be overlooked in the planning of a community engagement initiative. Responsible media coverage promotes the best interests of public schools. The "Reconnecting Communities and Schools" initiative in South Carolina, referred to earlier in this chapter, saw the media in a role as "committed observer," agreeing to report on the entire process without limiting coverage to only the "newsworthy" aspects (McDonnell & Weatherford, 1999). The community engagement process provides an opportunity to build and strengthen relationships with local media. These relationships are the key to responsible media coverage; a crisis is not the time to begin building relationships with the media.

The National School Public Relations Association provides some helpful guidelines for media relations (Armistead, 1999). School representatives should provide equal access to all local newspapers, radio, and television stations. Early in the relationship, they should provide reporters with basic written information about the district to ensure accuracy in future stories. It is a good idea to contact reporters with story ideas, while recognizing that only some of the stories will be used. In general, understanding the challenges of the reporter's job (i.e., deadlines) goes a long way toward building a mutually beneficial relationship. When planning a message, consider the target audience in determining content and format, avoiding the use of jargon. Honesty is also critically important; school officials should admit if they do not know the answer to a reporter's question. Phrases like "no comment" and "off the record" provoke suspicion. Credibility is incredibly difficult and time consuming to regain once it is lost. In a proactive relationship with the media, the positives will outweigh the negatives. The media can play a very important role in keeping the school district's other key constituencies informed. The 34th Annual Phi Delta Kappa/Gallup Poll provides evidence for this assertion, reporting that newspapers are the public's main source of information about schools (Rose & Gallup, 2002).

SOME HINTS FOR GETTING ORGANIZED

At this point, the task of getting the public involved may seem somewhat overwhelming. There are so many constituencies to consider. The grid shown in Table 3.1 can be used to summarize key information on constituents within the school system (administrators, teachers, etc.) and in the larger community (citizens, businesses, not-for-profits, etc.).

The type of grid can be used for internal analysis (with administrators, board members, teachers, and other staff as key constituencies) and for the community as a whole.

Let's consider an example. Parents, for instance, might be identified as an important constituency within the community, composed of several key subgroups. These might include the PTSA (Parents Teachers Students Association), parents of gifted/talented students, and parents of special needs students, among others. For each subgroup, their primary interests would be noted. Hypothetically speaking, let's assume the PTSA has as its primary focus increasing school funding and improving parent involvement. The parents of

Table 3.1   Constituency Analysis Grid

Constituency	Key Subgroups	Primary Interests re: Education	Overall Attitude re: Public Schools (using a 5-point scale)	Power Rating (using a 5-point scale)

gifted/talented students focus on college preparation and special programs like the International Baccalaureate and Advanced Placement. Parents of special needs students are interested in further improving the accessibility of public schools for their students.

Next we consider the overall attitude each of these subgroups has toward public schools. Is the subgroup generally positive regarding public schools or are they more negatively inclined? A five-point scale could be used here, where 5 = *very positive attitude*, 4 = *more positive than negative*, 3 = *neutral*, 2 = *more negative than positive*, and 1 = *very negative attitude*. Also important to consider is the relative power of each subgroup. How effective is this subgroup in promoting its agenda and in preventing action that would work against its agenda? Again, a five-point scale could be used, where 5 = *very powerful* and 1 = *not at all powerful*. This type of analysis will help those who initiate community engagement strategies to make sure that no important constituencies are overlooked. As the analysis progresses, educators may realize that they do not have all of the necessary information regarding constituencies, their interests, attitudes, and relative power. This may require some research to "fill in the gaps"; this topic will be addressed in the next chapter. Understanding where there is support within the community and where there may be resistance, while considering relative differences in power, can provide guidance in planning the amount of time each subgroup will require and then in designing the most effective approach for that subgroup. Subgroups that are supportive of public education can be leveraged to draw in other members of the community. Subgroups with negative attitudes will require extra time for listening to concerns in an attempt to find common ground.

The natural next step is to then think about connections and linkages with each of these constituencies and the associated subgroups. As educators, where do we have opportunities for dialogue with key constituencies? Who has a connection with various citizens' associations and not-for-profits within the community? Who has a connection with public institutions such as city government, law enforcement, hospitals, and libraries? Who has a connection with local business? Can we identify a "point person or persons" for each subgroup identified within our community? This "point person" need not be the superintendent or another member of the district central office team. Building principals, teachers, and support staff have a web of connections within the community as well. Make them a part of the community engagement effort. This broadens the reach of the engagement initiative and prevents the superintendent from feeling overwhelmed by the responsibility of making all of these contacts. Leveraging these connections will be explored in more detail in Chapter Five.

Now that key constituencies have been identified, the next task is to understand constituent expectations and perceptions regarding public schools. The public will begin to engage as its voice is heard. And with an understanding of constituent perspectives, educators will be more effective in their efforts to encourage public action to support public schools. A variety of techniques for exploring how constituents view public schools will be reviewed in the following chapter.

DISCUSSION QUESTIONS FOR CHAPTER 3

1. For each key internal constituency (board members, administrators, teachers, and staff):
   a. Is there support for the concept of community engagement? If not, what are the barriers to support?
   b. How can time be made available to facilitate this constituency's involvement in the community engagement process?

2. Using your analysis of external constituents summarized in Table 3.1:
   a. Sort constituent groups by those that are currently most engaged and those that are least engaged.
   b. For those groups that are more engaged, are there connections or expertise that can be leveraged in the development of the community engagement process?
   c. For those groups that are less engaged, are there known barriers that discourage further engagement?

Techniques to Better Understand Our Constituents

I have always been a strong supporter of public schools. My teenaged children are attending public school, I received a K–12 public school education, as did my parents. In the mid-1990s, I began working with Minnesota K–12 educators in a leadership development program funded by the Archibald Bush Foundation, a local foundation that promotes midcareer leadership education. As I listened to these educators share their challenges and their frustrations, I always found myself framing these issues from a marketing perspective. Because my undergraduate and graduate degrees are in marketing, this probably does not come as a great surprise! But I do believe that there is significant insight from marketing practice that can help educators in their efforts to engage the public.

CONSTITUENT ANALYSIS

In the previous chapter, we used a grid to identify internal and external constituencies, specifying key subgroups and their primary interests, attitudes toward public schools, and relative power (see Table 3.1). Internal constituencies for a school district would include the school board, administrators (district and building level), teachers, and support staff. Bridging the internal and external distinction are current students and their parents. Taxpayers within the community fund public schools; these taxpayers may be local businesses or individual citizens. The majority of these taxpayers will not have children currently enrolled in public schools. Not-for-profit organizations and public institutions, such as hospitals and law enforcement, also have a vested interest in public schools. While these organizations typically do not pay taxes, they may provide services to current students (i.e., libraries, social service agencies) or, in the longer term, they may hire these students as future employees.

Let's shift our focus to the typical situation faced by a business. Some of the important questions this business will ask include the following: *Who are our customers? What are their needs? Who are our competitors? How well do we satisfy customer needs relative to our competitors?* The essence of marketing involves maintaining the focus on satisfaction of customer needs, which, in turn, allows the firm to earn a profit. It's pretty tough for a firm to be profitable in the long run if it does a poor job of satisfying customer needs. The situation in education is considerably more complex. Who is the customer for the educational product? Certainly students would be considered customers. How about their parents? And what about the taxpayers who fund the education? And those who hire the product of a community's public school system?

In a business, the ultimate criterion used to judge any pending action is *profitability*. Although many other factors are likely to be considered, the profitability criterion does tend to simplify the process of evaluating alternative strategies and tactics. What is the ultimate criterion for decision making in education? Most would probably say *student achievement*. But how is that defined and measured? Again, the situation faced by educators is more complex than in most businesses.

The questions that guide businesses in their operations can still provide critical insight for public schools, however. While some may find the language of business to be offensive in an educational setting, there is value in understanding the needs and perspectives of the constituencies served by public schools. Harwood (2001) makes the argument that viewing public constituencies as "consumers" promotes self-interest at the expense of the common good, discourages a public sense of responsibility, and it shifts the focus to individual demands rather than common aspirations. Without question, public institutions like schools cannot be managed in the same way that a private enterprise would be managed. But failure to understand constituent perceptions of the value provided to them by this public institution results in a shortsightedness that may eventually threaten the institution's future. It may be necessary to educate the public on the value that all of us receive from strong public schools, such as increased property values, safer communities, and a more robust economy supported by a skilled workforce.

Additionally, citizens may need direction in how to look beyond self-interest to the interests of the larger community. But if citizens believe that they *personally* do not benefit from strong public schools, appealing to their sense of civic responsibility might not be sufficient to motivate commitment and action.

By addressing the following questions, educators will gain a greater understanding of the constituencies they serve. The answers to these questions may not be immediately evident and may thus require additional research. But the payoff will be well worth the effort, as the first step toward engaging the public.

- Who are our constituents (customers)?

This question was addressed as part of Table 3.1, where constituencies and the key subgroups within them were identified. Even though taxpayers may not be current users of the educational product (i.e., students and their parents), they still need to be included as an important constituency. And then there are key subgroups to be addressed within the taxpayer constituency, including local businesses and individual citizens. Although they are not considered taxpayers, not-for-profits and public institutions may have a vested interest in public schools as sources of future employees and as current recipients of their services (i.e., libraries, social service agencies, law enforcement).

- What are the expectations of our constituents, individually and collectively?

This is an area rich with insight. What need(s) does each constituency expect public schools to satisfy? Certainly, different constituencies may have different interests. Parents of students currently enrolled in public schools might desire that their children are prepared for college and are taught to become life-long learners, while local businesses are looking for public schools to train future employees who can come to work on time and make correct change. Exploring the question of constituent needs will likely lead to a discussion of the purpose of a public school education. As we saw in Chapter Two, there are many diverse perspectives on this issue. A community discussion on the purpose of a public school education can allow educators to do a better job of satisfying the community's needs by more effectively allocating scarce resources.

- Who are our competitors?

Public schools are facing unprecedented competition as the popularity of home schooling grows and as private schools may benefit from more widespread use of vouchers. Open enrollment means that public schools may also face competition from public schools in neighboring districts. How do the strengths and weaknesses of our school or district compare with the strengths and weaknesses of these other education alternatives? It is critical that we understand how our *constituents* perceive our strengths and weaknesses, as well as those of the competition. These perceptions may differ significantly from how we, as educators, would evaluate the strengths and weaknesses of our schools relative to the competition. Constituent *perception* is the reality with which we must work, no matter how misinformed or flawed it may be. It may be possible to educate our constituents so that their perceptions are more accurate, but current reality is the necessary starting point. We will also want to find out how many students we are losing annually to these competitors. In other words, what is the magnitude of the challenge presented by each competitor? This will determine if and how we will choose to respond to each competitive challenge.

- How well do public schools perform relative to other educational alternatives in the community?

Again, this is a question that should be answered by our constituents. Their perceptions may be dramatically different from our own. The overall level of performance can appear deceptively simple to assess, most often using a five-point scale where 5 = *outstanding* and 1 = *very poor.* But a numerical rating is limited in the amount of insight it can provide. What are the different dimensions of school performance? What factors are responsible for a lower-than-average evaluation of school performance? What sources of information does the constituent use in making this evaluation? How might a constituent's expectations influence his or her evaluation of school performance? These are just some of the questions that could provide richer understanding of constituent perceptions.

Another approach for evaluating our school or district relative to competition is to measure the constituents' perceived value of each educational alternative. Perceived value can be defined as follows:

$$\text{Perceived value} = \frac{\text{Perceived benefit of the educational alternative}}{\text{Perceived cost of the educational alternative}}$$

Thus, the concept of perceived value considers the cost of the alternative relative to the benefits received. While constituents might perceive that private schools offer greater benefits, they also realize that private schools come with a higher price tag. Public schools may thus receive a higher value rating, even though the level of perceived benefit is not as high.

Addressing these four questions will make educators more sensitive to the perceptions of their constituencies. With this insight, educators will be better able to design strategies that encourage constituents to share the responsibility of educating the community's children. As constituents find their voices being heard by local educators, they will be drawn into the community engagement process.

Techniques for Understanding Constituents

Without question, educators already have an abundance of data to manage. They have data on the demographic composition of their schools and the community at large. At a district or individual school level, they have data on test scores, along with a number of other variables including student enrollment, turnover, attendance, and so forth. But most school districts are still lacking good data on attitudes and perceptions held by key constituencies, which provide insight regarding changes in the variables they *do* monitor, such as enrollment and turnover. In order to design strategies that will be most effective in engaging a certain constituent group, educators must understand how those constituents currently perceive public schools. Four techniques, shown in Table 4.1, will be most useful to educators as they work to understand the views held by various constituent groups.

Focus groups and study circles work with smaller groups of constituents (fewer than 20 participants). Smaller groups may encourage some participants to express their views when a larger group setting would be intimidating. Focus groups typically deal with broad, open-ended questions, whereas study circles provide a set of specific questions (and

Table 4.1   Techniques for Understanding Constituents

Technique	Representation	Advantages	Limitations
Focus groups	Narrow—small group (fewer than 20 people)	• More comfortable for some participants • Open-ended discussions • Identifies issues that could derail a large-group meeting	• Not a representative sample of public opinion • Can be time consuming to hold multiple focus grous
Study circles	Narrow—small group (fewer than 20 people)	• More comfortable for some participants • Focused discussion on specific questions • Meets more than once	• Not a representative sample of public opinion • Can be time consuming
Surveys	Broad (large sample)	• Quantifiable • Can gather information quickly	• Limited depth of questioning • No opportunity for group discussion and feedback
Large-group events	Broad (up to several hundred people at a single event)	• Comprehensive view of public opinion • Opportunity for group discussion and consensus building	• Requires complex planning in advance of event • Event can be derailed by unanticipated conflict or hostility

accompanying data) for a well-defined issue. To accommodate larger numbers of participants at one time, educators may elect to use surveys or large-group events. Surveys can gather input from a broad cross-section of the population in a limited amount of time, but large-group events allow participants the opportunity to discuss the issues with one another in more depth. In the sections that follow, each technique will be presented in more detail, along with guidance on its appropriate use.

Focus Groups

A focus group is defined as a group of roughly 8 to 12 people who are led by a moderator in a guided but open-ended discussion of attitudes and perceptions related to a particular topic. Groups with more than 12 participants are harder to manage and may splinter into subgroups. Focus groups can be held with fewer than 8 participants, but smaller groups may not a yield a wide variety of opinions. Because focus groups are qualitative in nature, they provide insight and deeper understanding of participant attitudes and perceptions, but data gathered from focus groups is *not* statistically representative of the larger population. Successful focus groups are the result of careful planning, skilled implementation through use of a trained facilitator, and systematic analysis of the resulting data. Krueger (1994) and Jayanthi and Nelson (2002) offer excellent guides to the successful use of the focus group technique.

Study Circles and Related Techniques

Developed as a project of the Topsfield Foundation, a study circle is a group of 8 to 12 people who meet to discuss a public issue. They share perspectives in an attempt to find common ground and then move to a discussion of possible action. Typically, four two-hour sessions are scheduled, each addressing a particular aspect of the issue in question. The Study Circles Resource Center has created a discussion guide on education, as well as a number of other topics. Titled *Education: How Can Schools and Communities Work Together to Meet the Challenge?* (Leighninger & Niedergang, 1995b), the guide includes background information, a sampling of viewpoints on education, discussion questions, and examples of education initiatives from other communities. The guide also provides guidance on how to organize and moderate a study circle discussion. An abbreviated version, *The Busy Citizen's Discussion Guide: Education in Our Communities* (Leighninger & Niedergang, 1995a), presents the discussion questions in a format targeted toward participants. The four discussion sessions are organized as follows:

Session 1—How have schools affected our lives, and how do they affect our community?

Session 2—What do we want our graduates to know and to be able to do?

Session 3—Issues in education:

- How can we meet every student's needs?
- How can we make our schools safer?
- How can we deal with racial and ethnic diversity?
- How can we provide a quality education with limited resources?

Session 4—Making a difference: What can we do in our community?

Study circles can be implemented on a larger scale, with multiple study circles in operation at any time. Typically, however, discussions are limited to within an individual study circle, not shared between study circles. For more information on organizing and facilitating study circles, contact the Study Circles Resource Center, 697 Pomfret Street, Pomfret, CT 06258; phone: (860) 928–2616; *www.studycircles.org*.

National Issues Forums

National Issues Forums bring citizens together to discuss important issues that include education, the economy, health care, foreign affairs, poverty, and crime—similar to study circles. These discussions can take place in small- or large-group settings. Typically, the larger groups (more than 20) meet only once, whereas the smaller groups may meet on several occasions. The National Issues Forums Institute, working in conjunction with Public Agenda and the Kettering Foundation, has developed a series of discussion guides on a wide variety of topics. For education, they offer *Public Schools: Is There a Way to Fix Them?* (National Issues Forums, 1999b). As the basis for stimulating discussion, this guide presents four different approaches to improving public schools:

1. Give parents a choice of schools.

2. Raise academic standards and stress the basics.

3. Make education a community effort.

4. Provide adequate funds to all schools.

Participants have the opportunity to discuss the strengths and shortcomings of each approach while searching for common ground on the way toward some type of public action. To assist convenors and moderators of National Issues Forums, a guide titled *Organizing for Public Deliberation and Moderating a Forum/Study Circle* (1999a) is available. For more information, contact Public Agenda, 6 E. 39th St., New York, NY 10016; www.publicagenda.org/aboutpa/aboutpa4.htm.

Community Conversations

Community conversations are part of a larger initiative offered by the Harwood Institute—whose mission is to work with people who want to take responsibility for improving public life and politics—entitled "Reconnecting Communities and Schools." "Reconnecting" consists of four phases stretching over a two-year period: start-up; community engagement; public action; and sustaining and accountability. The community engagement phase includes open meetings in a large-group format, community conversations using smaller discussion groups, and the creation of "compacts" to specify the joint commitment of schools and the community to take future action. For those communities that cannot accommodate a two-year process, the Harwood Institute (2000a) has developed a stand-alone kit on the use of community conversations.

Community conversations make use of discussion groups with no more than 15 participants. Four sessions are scheduled to address the following themes: (1) imagine the community and education we want, (2) identify the challenges we face, (3) figure out ways to act, and (4) agree to take action (The Harwood Institute, 2000a). The "Community Conversations" kit provides detailed instructions on how to find an appropriate venue, how to recruit participants, and how to moderate the discussions. For more information, contact the Harwood Institute, 4915 St. Elmo Avenue, Suite 402, Bethesda, MD 20814; *www.theharwoodinstitute.org*.

Fishbowl Conversations

A variation on the use of small-group discussion comes from the Native American culture. In the "fishbowl" are two sets of circles, one for speakers and one for listeners. Six speakers and a moderator sit in the inner circle, which includes two empty chairs. The outer circle is composed of listeners who must move to one of the two chairs in order to ask clarifying questions. Otherwise, the listeners are not allowed to join the conversation until it is their turn to join the inner circle of speakers. This technique is especially effective, when it is appropriate, to force participants to listen to viewpoints that are different from their own. Educators have also found that the fishbowl technique works particularly well for soliciting input from students. The Paterson Education

Fund in New Jersey has extensive experience with fishbowl conversations. For more information, contact the Paterson Education Fund in Paterson, New Jersey; phone: (973) 881-8914; *www.paterson-education.org.*

Planning Small-Group Discussions

Use of the small-group discussion technique requires some advance planning. This responsibility can be assumed by the planning team described in Chapter Two or by another designated group that adequately represents key constituencies within the community. The format for the small-group discussions needs to be determined, along with the number of groups that can be accommodated, consistent with time and budget constraints.

Next, dates and sites for the discussions should be selected. Meeting places should be welcoming, comfortable, and accessible to a broad cross-section of the community. Arrangements for refreshments, child care, and any necessary equipment (flip charts, video and audio recorders, etc.) also need to be made.

In addition, moderators, recorders, and interpreters need to be selected and trained, if necessary. Critical to the success of the discussion, moderators can probe for more insight, make sure key questions are addressed, and keep the group focused. Moderators should have group facilitation skills and some knowledge of education issues, and they should be perceived as nonpartisan. Experienced moderators can often be found in local businesses, community agencies, or higher education. In the event that experienced moderators are not readily available, training can be sought from experts or published sources. If the discussions will not be recorded using audio or video technology, then arrangements must be made for a person, separate from the moderator, to take notes. Notes or tapes will be forwarded to the planning team upon completion of the discussions. Interpreters should be provided for all participants whose native language is not English.

Moderators need to be provided with an interview guide to lead the discussion. If appropriate, the planning team can select one of the published guides from the Study Circles Resource Center, the National Issues Forums, or the Harwood Institute. If a more customized approach is necessary, then it is the planning committee's responsibility to design the interview guide and make copies available to the moderators.

Community members should be invited to participate in the discussions at least two weeks before the meetings are scheduled to occur. All key constituencies should be included, as discussed in Chapter Three. Contact local businesses, neighborhood associations, faith communities, clubs, and other interest groups to make sure that a variety of perspectives are represented in each discussion. Educators may be included in the discussion groups as long as they do not constitute a majority of the participants or otherwise dominate the discussion. Personal contact via the telephone or face-to-face interaction is typically more effective in recruitment than mass mailings. Phone trees can be used to spread the calling responsibility among a larger group. Those who agree to participate can be asked to recommend others who might be interested, but it is best to avoid assigning friends or family members to the same group. It may be necessary to overrecruit constituencies that are likely to be underrepresented. As community members agree to participate, this information should be recorded so that a diverse representation of the community can be assigned to each discussion group and extra efforts can be made to recruit underrepresented constituencies. One or two days before the scheduled discussion, a phone reminder is an effective way to ensure that the groups are well attended.

One final issue to be addressed by the planning team concerns the issue of observers. Is media coverage appropriate for these discussions, and, if so, what are the ground rules for media involvement? School board members, the district superintendent, and elected officials may also be included as observers of the community discussions. The planning team will need to be clear in specifying the role that observers are to play. The opportunity to hear citizens talk about the public schools can be very powerful for local school and municipal officials. These observers can also offer their insight and evaluation after the discussions have occurred.

Survey Research

As noted in the previous section, one limitation of qualitative research is that the resulting data is not statistically representative of the population at large. A survey, making use of a randomly selected sample of respondents, is necessary to estimate the frequency associated with perceptions, opinions, and behaviors. Due to the quantitative emphasis of survey research, the data obtained will not be able to provide the richness and depth of insight found in more qualitative methodologies. Quantitative and qualitative approaches complement one another and together provide a more complete picture of the population of interest.

Survey research is characterized by a systematic approach to data collection. It is important for the users of survey data to be familiar with the process that was used to collect the data. In some cases, it may be possible to design and implement a survey without the assistance of a professional research consultant. When additional expertise is needed, research vendors may be consulted. If budgets are tight, a more cost-effective strategy would involve the use of faculty and/or students from a local college or university to provide the needed research assistance. Larger businesses in the community may also be willing to offer their research capabilities. For more information on the survey research process, good references are provided by Alreck and Settle (1994), Cox (1996), and Thomas (1999).

Large-Group Events

Town Meetings

Public Agenda makes use of a town meeting framework when conducting its community conversations on education. As an example, in collaboration with the Institute for Educational

Leadership, Public Agenda hosted a series of town meetings on education in the mid-1990s (Danzberger & Friedman, 1997). In each community where a town meeting was held, between 75 and 100 community members participated. The basic structure of a town meeting consists of an initial plenary session to welcome all participants and set the ground rules. Then, participants break into smaller groups of 15 to 20 members from different constituencies. Typically, these smaller groups move into breakout rooms, if available, to discuss the issue of interest with the assistance of a group moderator and a recorder. Later, all participants come back to a central location to share findings and discuss future action. Most town meetings last approximately four hours, with a light lunch or dinner served. While the time commitment may seem a bit overwhelming at first, most participants left the meetings with the feeling that they needed more time (Danzberger & Friedman, 1997).

One of the advantages of the town meeting format is that it can be easily modified to fit the characteristics of the situation. An interesting use of this format, although not directly related to public schools, occurred in late July 2002, when approximately 5,000 residents of New York City and the surrounding area came together in the Jacob K. Javits Convention Center to discuss six development plans for the World Trade Center site. Participants included families of September 11 victims, neighborhood residents, local businesses, and commercial developers. Each constituency brought its own vision of the future for the World Trade Center site, along with their concerns about the rebuilding process. Planners and local officials heard the need to memorialize this site in addition to restoring the lost commercial and retail space to some degree. The consensus was that the design process should be extended to address these concerns (Visions of Ground Zero, 2002).

Future Search Conference

As the name implies, a Future Search Conference is oriented to the future, helping people with divergent perspectives to share insight, understand the need for change, and formulate action plans (Bunker & Alban, 1997). Developers Marvin Weisbord and Sandra Janoff wanted to design a technique that would bring "the whole system into the room" (quoted in Bunker & Alban, 1997, p. 44) to create a shared vision for the future, along with action plans to make it happen. The emphasis is on finding common ground, first within self-managing tables of eight participants each, and then as a larger group. Weisbord and Janoff believe the ideal number of participants for a Future Search Conference is between 70 and 80. This number assures a diversity of perspectives, while preserving a sense of community. From a practical standpoint, this size is more manageable, since each table shares its work with the larger group. If more participants need to be accommodated, several Future Search Conferences can be run simultaneously.

A Future Search Conference is designed to take place over a three-day time period (Bunker & Alban, 1997). The first day focuses on the history of the organization or community, leading up to the present and a discussion of current trends. The second day starts with a discussion of what participants feel proud about and sorry about in relation to the main theme of the conference. Each stakeholder group begins to see itself as part of a larger system. This leads into a brainstorming session to design the "ideal" future. Each table completes this task, and then common themes are recorded as each table shares its vision for the future. The third day focuses on the development of action plans to address these common themes. Also addressed are the plans for communication and follow-up after the conference has ended. Participants will not want to lose the momentum gained during the conference.

The three-day format allows for what Weisbord calls "soak time" at the end of each day. Weisbord and Janoff recommend that the conference start around midday on the first day and end at midday on the third day. Understandably, some may feel that this type of time commitment is not realistic for their particular community. Some Future Search Conferences have been compressed into a two-day time period, but participants may find their energy levels drained when it is time to start action planning. If time is an issue, another large-group methodology with a less ambitious agenda may be a better fit. An excellent resource is the book *Large Group Interventions: Engaging the Whole System for Rapid Change* by Barbara Benedict Bunker and Billie T. Alban (1997). They describe the different large-group methodologies in detail, highlighting the differences between methods and when each is most appropriately used. In addition, the International Association for Public Participation offers a comprehensive set of courses for facilitators and planners of large-group events. For specific training in the Future Search Conference methodology, the book by Weisbord and Janoff (1995) titled *Future Search* offers a comprehensive "how-to" guide.

Planning a Large-Group Event

In many ways, planning a large-group discussion event is quite similar to planning for small-group discussions. Logistics will play a more critical role in large-group discussions, because more people are involved and the flow of events may be more complex. Discussions occurring in smaller groups around tables somehow need to be shared with the larger community. Once again, a planning team will be responsible for addressing the following issues:

1. Carefully assess the situation.
   - Establish a time line.
   - Determine budget for the large group event.
   - Evaluate the "political" climate—assess the level of stakeholder support and resistance to the discussion issue.
   - Clearly define the issue and desired outcomes from the event.

(See Table 4.2 for a list of possible topics to be discussed.)

Table 4.2   Possible Large-Group Discussion Topics

- Strategic planning/creating a vision for public schools
- The purpose of a public school education and implications for resource allocation
- Standards development and implementation
- School funding
- Strategies to encourage parent and community involvement
- Improving achievement of all students

2. Secure the facility for the large-group event and set the date.
   - The site should be neutral, welcoming, comfortable, and accessible to all.
   - The site should have plenty of parking spaces, adequate restrooms, numerous electrical outlets, walls that can accommodate tape or other adhesives, and breakout rooms, if needed.
   - Arrange for round tables that can seat eight participants at each.
   - Arrange for child care and transportation for those who need it.
   - Determine who will provide the meal for the event.

3. Recruit and train facilitators; hire interpreters

4. Design the event and create discussion guide. (See Table 4.3 for a sample design of a four-hour event.)
   - Alternate between small-group discussions at round tables and with the larger community as a whole.
   - Allow time to summarize input from each round table
   - Frame education issues as alternatives or choices as opposed to discussing an open-ended issue. (Public Agenda found this to be very helpful.)
   - Create handouts of school data or other information to be used by discussion participants (if applicable).
   - Specify all materials needed for the event (name tents, easel pads, markers, audiovisual equipment, etc.).

Table 4.3   Sample Design of a Four-Hour Large-Group Event on the Topic of Student Achievement

15 minutes	Introduction/ground rules
90 minutes	How should we define student achievement in our community? • Brief overview by facilitator (5 minutes) • Group discussion at each round table (40 minutes) • Large-group sharing of table results (30 minutes) • Large-group facilitator summary (15 minutes)
15 minutes	Break and serve meal, to be eaten during the next discussion
90 minutes	What action should be taken to improve student achievement in our community? • Brief overview by facilitator (5 minutes) • Group discussion at each round table (40 minutes) • Large-group sharing of table results (45 minutes)
30 minutes	Large-group facilitator summary of action plans and next steps

5. Recruit participants at least two weeks in advance.
   • The number of contacts required is approximately three times larger than the desired number of participants; that is, one must make 1,500 contacts in order to recruit 500 participants (O'Callaghan Jr., 1999a).
   • Overrecruit groups that are likely to be underrepresented.
   • No more than 20% of participants should be school professionals.

- Use personal referrals to identify possible participants.
- Assign confirmed participants to tables, assuring diverse representation at each.
- Use a phone tree to make reminder calls one to two days before the event.

6. Contact local media regarding coverage of the event.

7. Plan the event follow-up.
   - Will participants complete a post-event evaluation?
   - Who will send thank-you notes to all participants?
   - How will participants receive information about action taken as a result of their input?
   - Will participants have an opportunity to take part in future action?

For more detailed information on planning large-group events, William O'Callaghan Jr. (1999a) has prepared a planning manual based on his community engagement consulting experience (which he calls his public engagement experience) with school districts in Ohio. It includes specific recruitment strategies, a community-meeting checklist, hints for working with the local media, and an appendix filled with sample invitations, press releases, and feedback forms. Another excellent resource for planning community discussions is *Quality Now! Results of National Conversations on Education and Race*, a joint project of the Public Education Network and Public Agenda (2000). It features a tool kit for planning, publicizing, and evaluating community discussions.

DEVELOPING A DATA MANAGEMENT SYSTEM

Most organizations complain about having *too much* data, rather than not having enough. Schools are certainly no different. Data are already collected on daily attendance, per-pupil funding, test scores, enrollments, and graduation rates, and the list continues. As schools begin to collect new data on constituent attitudes, perceptions, and expectations, some type of mechanism will be necessary for organizing and disseminating this information to others who can use it. Computers are a huge asset in organizing information so that it can be useful to others. It is also helpful if an employee at both the district and building level can be designated with the responsibility for data management so that others know whom to contact with questions. Meetings at the building and district level can be used as a forum for sharing the latest research results and discussing the implications. Greater insight and more effective policy decisions are possible only if the necessary information is easily accessible to those who can make use of it. In the next chapter, we will see how understanding the perspectives held by key constituencies allows educators to do a better job of connecting with the community.

DISCUSSION QUESTIONS FOR CHAPTER 4

1. Which technique or combination of techniques is most appropriate for gathering additional insight on the perceptions and expectations held by various constituent groups in our community?

   Factors to be considered include:
   - Time and budget constraints
   - The issue to be addressed
   - Need for open-ended versus structured questions
   - Total number of people who need to be involved
   - Diversity of opinion; potential for conflict
   - Constituent preferences

2. Who will plan these data collection efforts? The overall planning team for the community engagement process or a designated subcommittee?

3. Whom can we consult for further guidance on the use of this technique? Web sites? Local or regional experts from the public or private sector? University faculty?

4. Are there members of the community who have skills to share in leading group discussions? Tabulating and analyzing data? Can these skills be used to leverage resources available through the school district?

5. Are there organizations or individuals within the community who would be willing to provide partial or complete funding for data collection activities?

6. How will we share this acquired insight with those who can use the information?

Strategies
to Encourage
Constituent Action

In this chapter, we will focus on strategies for building and strengthening bridges with constituencies that are not fully engaged with public schools. Greater understanding of these constituencies may be accomplished by using some of the techniques presented in the previous chapter or through informal conversations with members of the community. Leadership at the school district and building level will be critical to the success of any engagement initiative. Superintendents and principals will work with others in establishing the vision of what an engaged public could do for public schools, and then will provide direction and encouragement to community members as they work to make it happen. While many school districts have a designated community relations position, it is unrealistic to expect one person, typically with limited line authority, to successfully engage the community as a solo effort. Every person who works in the public schools has a role to play in creating a welcoming environment within the schools. These same people serve as ambassadors for the schools as they interact with others outside the school environment.

MOVING OUT FROM THE
SCHOOL INTO THE COMMUNITY

A common complaint among educators deals with the low attendance at open houses and other opportunities for the public to visit schools. A superintendent might say, "I have a designated time each week for having coffee with the community and no one shows up." Principals and teachers may complain that even parents of current students do not attend conferences and other school events in any large numbers. Unfortunately, the reality is that the public is currently disengaged, for a variety of reasons that were addressed in Chapter One. We can spend a lot of time thinking about how the public *should* be more involved, but that doesn't address the current reality. As educators, we need to reach out and meet our constituents where they are, not where we would like them to be. And that may require educators to move out from the public schools into the community as a necessary first step.

All school employees can reach out to the public through their day-to-day interactions with community members outside of the school environment. Whether it is a friendly chat while waiting in line at the local supermarket or joining the conversation at the hair salon or barbershop, educators can connect with citizens in many different locations. In these more informal settings, it is often easier for citizens to share their concerns about public schools. Some school administrators make a habit of conducting regular "brown bag lunch" discussions at local businesses. Educators are also members of many diverse organizations within the community, including service clubs (i.e., Rotary, Kiwanis, etc.), community organizations (i.e., scout troops, intramural athletics, etc.), and faith communities. These settings also provide many opportunities for informal conversations.

As educators prepare for these informal conversations, it is helpful to become aware of the assumptions they have about their community. All of us operate using assumptions about people, organizations, and how systems work. Assumptions allow us to function by simplifying an extraordinarily complex world. But sometimes assumptions can become a barrier between us and the community we seek to engage. Educators receive most of their feedback from those who have complaints or problems; it is easy to see why they might become jaded and assume that the entire community shares these negative opinions. The Harwood Institute (2000c) has developed a "Professionalism Barometer" kit as part of their initiative titled "Reconnecting Communities and Schools." The "Professionalism Barometer" is designed to help educators identify their key assumptions about the community, understand how these assumptions influence their decision making, determine which assumptions need to change, and track progress in changing these assumptions. Without the burden of these problematic assumptions, educators are better able to hear the true opinions of community members.

As a whole, this network of connections between educators and community members can be used as a source of ongoing intelligence about public sentiment toward the schools. As issues of concern are identified, they can be further explored using techniques like focus groups and surveys, which were addressed in the previous chapter. In order to make use of this network, a database can be built, containing voluntary information on each school employee's connections within the community. A form for collecting this information from individual educators can be found in Table 5.1. This information would then be very helpful in leveraging those connections when face-to-face communication with the community is needed.

Educators at all levels, not just the district superintendent, will want to pursue opportunities to "tell their story" to interested groups. We sometimes forget how extensively schools are intertwined within the life of the community. Schools are employers who can hire local residents and organizational

Table 5.1   Community Involvement Form for Educators

	Officer—Past or Present	Hours Per Month
Service clubs, such as Lions, Rotary, Kiwanis		
Chamber of Commerce, Jaycees, etc.		
Veterans groups such as VFW, American Legion, etc.		
Farm organizations or co-ops		
PTA, PTSA, PTO		
Leader of youth clubs (scouts, 4-H, etc.)		
Charitable organizations (United Way, Red Cross, American Cancer Society, etc.)		
Political parties or groups		
Women of Today, AAUW, League of Women Voters, etc.		
Church councils or committees		
Senior citizens groups		
Economic or civic development associations		
Appointed community committees or advisory groups		
Law enforcement volunteers		
Volunteer emergency services		
Other		

purchasers who can support local vendors, and each school employee is an individual consumer who has the opportunity to support local business. Supporting local business should be encouraged as an easy way of building trust and support within the local community. This may be less feasible in urban and suburban districts where larger numbers of school employees may live outside of the school district. Educators should also be encouraged to ask for the opportunity to speak to local groups with whom they are affiliated. This will make it easier for the speaker to know his or her audience and tailor remarks to their specific concerns. Educators can share stories of progress the schools have made and the vision of possibilities for the future. The Harwood Institute (2000b) offers a tool on "Generating a New Public Story" with helpful hints on how to generate an authentic and meaningful public story and then how to actively manage it over time. The National School Public Relations Association also has a number of resources on this topic.

Visibility and effective communication are critically important within the political arena. Encourage all school employees to get to know their local school board members, city and county officials, and state legislators. Invite these elected officials into the schools, so they can see education policy in action. School administrators can leverage their knowledge of community sentiment regarding education to work more effectively within the political arena. Understanding current public opinion through use of the techniques addressed in Chapter Four will allow the administrator to be proactive and seize the best opportunity to push for needed change. According to the National Association of Elementary School Principals (2001), educators can be most effective in shaping education legislation when they mobilize coalitions composed of individual and group constituents. A bipartisan approach that offers solutions and is research based has a much greater chance of success than a collection of educator complaints.

Bringing the Community Into the Schools

Certainly, there is value in using educators as ambassadors of the schools in the greater community. But ultimately, the goal is to bring the public into the schools so they can understand firsthand the challenges facing today's educators and then can more fully support the schools in terms of time, talent, and money. It may have been years since most citizens have been in a school building during a typical day. Several years ago, I asked the members of my church's senior citizens group if they would be interested in volunteering at the local elementary school. It had never occurred to them that they could be useful by reading to children or just spending some one-on-one time with a child who needs some extra attention. Teachers embraced the idea, welcoming the presence of an extra adult in the classroom. A nucleus of six to eight seniors began volunteering, and not long afterward, they would look for me on Sunday mornings at church. The typical reaction was "I had no idea that teachers had to deal with so many different challenges! School is so different than when I was a student sixty years ago!" One woman had spent a morning with a young girl who had recently emigrated from Russia and was unable to speak English. Experiences like these had a profound impact on the seniors at my church and play an important role in promoting understanding and building support for public schools.

It is easy to become frustrated when invitations to the community are extended and no one shows up. The natural response would be to give up. But educators will ultimately see results if they persist in their attempts to engage the community. It may be helpful to return to the value equation from the previous chapter (p. 55):

$$\text{Perceived value of involvement} = \frac{\textit{Perceived benefit from involvement}}{\textit{Perceived cost of involvement}}$$

Educators can gain valuable insight from understanding a constituent's perspective regarding involvement. If a constituent does not perceive that the benefits received from involvement exceed the cost of involvement, he or she will not be motivated to take the necessary action to become involved. This is true for a parent deciding whether to attend a child's conference, a citizen deciding whether to volunteer at a school, or a voter deciding whether to support a bond or levy referendum.

Thus there are two basic strategies available to alter perception of value: increase the level of perceived benefit or decrease the level of perceived cost. For example, some taxpayers may not see the direct benefit of investing in public schools. Economists are now beginning to address the financial return associated with dollars invested in education. In 2003 the Federal Reserve Bank in Minneapolis completed a study that identified a 12% estimated real internal rate of return associated with investment in early childhood programs that target children living in poverty. The public benefits of this investment include more efficient K–12 education, increased worker productivity, and a decrease in crime and welfare payments (Rolnick & Grunewald, 2003). Attempts can also be made to reduce the real or perceived costs associated with a particular action. We will see examples of both benefit-enhancement and cost-reduction strategies as the issues of parent involvement, community involvement, and shared decision making are addressed in the remainder of this chapter.

Parent Involvement

Thirty years of research has shown that parents and other family members who are involved in a child's education will have a significant positive impact on that child's school attendance, completion of homework, grades, performance on tests, graduation from high school, and interest in attending college (Henderson & Berla, 1994; Henderson & Mapp, 2002; U.S. Department of Education, 1994). As a result, most schools are interested in increasing family involvement, especially those who serve large populations of at-risk students. Joyce Epstein (1995), director of the Center on School, Family, and

Community Partnerships at Johns Hopkins University, has developed a framework for understanding the different types of cooperation between families, schools, and the community. The six dimensions she has identified are:

1. *Parenting.* Families must provide a healthy and safe environment at home that promotes learning and good behavior at school. Schools can provide information and training to support families in this endeavor.

2. *Communicating.* Families need information about school programs and student progress in a format that meets their individual needs.

3. *Volunteering.* Families can make significant contributions to the school, if schools can accommodate their schedules and interests.

4. *Learning at home.* Families can facilitate and supervise learning at home with the assistance of teachers.

5. *Decision making.* Families can have meaningful roles in the school decision-making process. This opportunity should be made available to all members of the community, not just those who have the most time and energy to devote.

6. *Collaboration with the community.* Schools can help families gain access to support services from other community agencies (i.e., health care, child care, etc.). Schools can also help mobilize families and other community groups in efforts to improve community life (i.e., recycling programs, food banks).

The National PTA has developed standards for parent/ family involvement programs using Epstein's six dimensions. The standards include criteria to be considered in creating successful parent/family involvement programs (National PTA, 2000). In addition, the National PTA has crafted surveys, forms, and worksheets for parents and educators to use in addressing key issues related to involvement (National PTA, 2000, Appendices B and C). Many of these resources can also be found on the National PTA Web site (*www.pta.org*).

However, there are some very real barriers that prevent families from being more involved in their children's education. According to a report by the U.S. Department of Education, these barriers include (1) lack of time and/or money, (2) lack of information or training, (3) differences in perceptions or values, and (4) issues with school space and facilities (Funkhouser, Gonzales, & Moles, 1997). Each of these barriers will be examined in more detail in the sections that follow, along with specific strategies to address each barrier.

Lack of Time and/or Money

Busy schedules are typical of modern life in America. Most parents find themselves pressed for time. For low-income families, the challenges can often be overwhelming. Money is tight, and adults may be working more than one job to make ends meet. If schools can be sensitive and responsive to these concerns, parents can have the opportunity and the motivation to initiate communication and to attend more school events. Administrators must also be sensitive to the demands on teachers' time. Reaching out to parents takes time that somehow must be made available. Some of the strategies schools have used include:

- Providing transportation to school events.
- Offering meals and child care in conjunction with school events.
  (Older students can provide assistance with childcare.)
- Making teachers available outside the school to meet with parents before the school day begins.
- Accommodating parent drop-ins by using the principal or another teacher to cover the classroom.
- Using mobile learning units to bring teachers and learning resources to neighborhoods.

- Scheduling neighborhood meetings with parents and school representatives in a home or public place.
- Encouraging teachers to make home visits when possible. These visits, and observing a student's home environment, can provide rich insight.

In order to make time available to teachers for these activities, schools have used some creative approaches. These include release time for teachers, freeing teachers from responsibilities during lunch, early dismissals to allow for committee work and program planning, providing a daily in-school planning period, and offering stipends or compensatory time off (Funkhouser et al., 1997).

Lack of Information or Training

Once the barriers of time and money have been addressed, parents need simple information about school events. They also need information on how well their child is doing in school. In order to be effective in supporting their child's learning at home or to become a volunteer, they may need additional training. Some of the strategies schools have used to address information and training needs include:

- Using multiple modalities for communication—mail, telephone, word-of-mouth, local newspapers, and radio stations.
- Scheduling a monthly forum for school administrators to hear parent concerns.
- Inviting parents into their child's classroom to observe and learn new techniques for facilitating learning at home and at school.
- Using telephone trees in which each parent calls some designated number of other families to announce events and encourage attendance. Parents calling other parents can sometimes be more effective than educators calling parents.

- Offering translation for all communication, addressing all languages spoken in the parent population. One New Mexico school used the local AM radio station that broadcasts in Navajo to announce school events (Funkhouser et al., 1997).
- Hosting Family Nights in math, science, and technology to engage older students and to train parents in how to facilitate more technical learning at home.
- Training parents for volunteer work and homework help, and for supporting learning in general at home.
- Training teachers on how to more effectively engage parents.

Differences in Perceptions and Values

Schools can provide all the necessary information and training, while making involvement convenient and cost-effective, and still parents may not participate. Remember the value equation? The value associated with participation is calculated as the ratio of perceived benefit to perceived cost. The time, money, and information issues deal with cost to participate. But what about parents' perceptions of the benefits associated with being involved in their child's education? As educators, we believe that all parents should want to be involved in their child's school because it is the right thing to do. We have thirty years of research to prove it! But parents may not see it that way for a variety of reasons. Parents may simply not know how important their involvement is to their child's success in school. They may lack education themselves or have bad memories of their own school experiences, or they may dread hearing about a child who is performing poorly at school. The following are strategies used by schools to increase the perceived benefit associated with family involvement:

- Offering food and entertainment (both can be donated) in conjunction with school events. Humboldt Senior High School in St. Paul, Minnesota, hosted a Family Fun

Night to inform students about planning for college. A mariachi band played background music, a local Mexican mercado catered the meal, and participants played games like "I'm Going to College" bingo where they learned words related to college planning.

- Creating positive, fun events to balance parent-teacher conferences that may be viewed by parents as a forum for bad news. These events include awards assemblies, carnivals, and so forth.
- Building parent interest by incorporating student performance into the school event. (Every parent likes to see his or her child perform!)
- Combining open houses and parent meetings with athletic events to generate parent interest.
- Contacting parents with good news about their students as well as any bad news.
- Recognizing the impact of culture on parental attitudes. For example, in the Hispanic culture, teachers are so highly regarded that parents are comfortable entrusting their child's education solely to teachers (Funkhouser et al., 1997).
- Focusing on the parents' personal and professional development. Some schools offer workshops on résumé writing, interview skills, and computer skills in conjunction with school events. Other schools work with community organizations to provide health care services and general equivalency diploma (GED) preparation. Schools can work with immigrant parents to help them gain citizenship status. The Logan Square Neighborhood Association in Chicago developed a mentor program for parents, where the goal is the parent's personal development. The program provides training, the opportunity to assist for 100 hours in the classroom, and a stipend upon completion of the program (Jehl, Blank, & McCloud, 2001).
- Offering specific incentives for parent involvement. Some schools require a compact to be signed by teachers,

students, and parents at the beginning of the term. At Turnbull Learning Academy in San Mateo, California, parents track participation through a point system. They earn a designated number of points for helping with homework, attending school events, and completing weekly literacy activities with their children (Funkhouser et al., 1997).

Issues with School Space and Facilities

Schools can do all the work to bring parents into the school, only to offer them a less-than-friendly welcome when they arrive. If parent involvement is to be sustained, it is the school's responsibility to create a welcoming and personalized environment with dedicated space for parents. Here are some strategies that schools have used to address this issue:

- Making the first impression more positive by replacing the infamous "Report to the Office" sign with a "Welcome" sign. Some schools designate an alternate entrance for parents rather than subject them to elaborate security measures each time they enter.
- Creating a more personalized environment through the "schools within a school" concept. By using teams or pods, schools seem smaller and more accessible.
- Setting aside space for parents in the school building. The term "family center" is often used for this space. It is typically an informal lounge where parent workshops and PTA meetings can be held. Some schools locate the teacher workspace in the family center so parents can help teachers with projects or share lunch, facilitating interaction between teachers and parents. Furniture and other material resources can be donated by local business. At Cane Run Elementary School in Louisville, Kentucky, funds from the 1990 Kentucky Education Reform Act provided for a Family Resource Center that serves the entire community. A full-time coordinator

links families with mental health counseling, medical services, social services, and other community services. Clothes and food are collected for families in need. Volunteers provide transportation when needed, and the center even pays the GED testing fee! The center also provides an affordable afterschool program at $10 per week (Funkhouser et al., 1997).

The ideas presented here are only a sampling of the many successful approaches used by schools to encourage parent involvement. An excellent resource on strategies for improving parent involvement is a National PTA publication titled *Building Successful Partnerships: A Guide for Developing Parent and Family Involvement Programs* (2000). While there is little doubt that family involvement is critical to student achievement, the larger community can also make a meaningful contribution to the education of our children.

Community Involvement

While most educators acknowledge the need to spend time encouraging parents to become more involved in their child's education, they may balk at allocating time to involve the greater community. The demands on an educator's time are already intense; each new initiative requires more time, and rarely are existing responsibilities modified to make room for new ones. Clearly, a significant cost is associated with building stronger school-community relationships. But the benefit to be gained from these stronger relationships must also be considered. If community members have a stronger relationship with public schools built upon mutual understanding and trust, then they are more likely to support public schools. This support may come in a financial form, through contributions or willingness to pay higher taxes, or in the form of time spent volunteering. Once again, the value equation is relevant: What is the perceived cost relative to the perceived benefit to be gained? Time invested in building school-community relationships can pay big dividends to public schools.

Schools can use a number of strategies to strengthen relationships with the larger community. The main objective underlying all of these strategies is to get people into the schools! At any given point in time, the majority of the community will *not* have a child currently enrolled in public school. It may have been years since an individual has had any personal contact with the public schools. That personal connection is the foundation of a strong relationship. This can happen through community education programs, use of school buildings for community activities, volunteer opportunities, and partnerships between schools and community organizations.

Community Education

Community education programs recognize that learning occurs throughout life, both inside and outside schools. These programs may include early childhood education, extended-day and enrichment programs for school-age children, adult education, leisure activities, workforce preparation, and vocational training (Decker, 2001). Many school districts offer community education programs but may not leverage these contacts as a source of support for public schools. Because they already have a connection with the school district, participants in community education programs can be seen as potential volunteers and likely supporters of tax initiatives to fund schools. They may also be asked to advocate for public schools within their own personal circles of influence.

Use of School Buildings for Community Activities

Public schools offer physical facilities, such as computer labs, meeting rooms, gyms, and playgrounds, that can accommodate nonschool activities. This provides another opportunity for the public to come in contact with public schools, in addition to providing the school district with more cost-effective use of its facilities. Schools can serve as polling places, sites for intramural athletics, meeting locations for scout troops, and a host of other community activities. In Cloquet, Minnesota, planning is under way to make the recreational facilities at the middle school available to the community in the form of an activity center. In Rochester, New York, new schools are being built with dedicated space for community organizations (Jehl et al., 2001). This is an example of an increasingly popular vision of schools as the center of the community, giving rise to the concept of a community school. According to the Coalition for Community Schools (2000, p. 2), "A community school, operating in a public school building, is open to students, families, and the community before, during, and after school, seven days a week, all year long." Community schools typically include family support centers to help families with child rearing, employment, housing, and other services. Medical, dental, and mental health services are also readily accessible. Stanley Elementary School in Wichita, Kansas, is generally open and in use from 7 A.M. to midnight, seven days a week. The school houses substations of the city's departments of Health, Human Resources, and Parks and Recreation, in addition to a library and a senior service center. During evenings and weekends, the school hosts college classes, community programs, and recreation for adults (Coalition for Community Schools, 2000). Stronger school-community relationships are the result of using public schools as the hub of the community.

Volunteer Opportunities

According to Marian Wright Edelman, founder and director of the Children's Defense Fund, volunteering is "the rent we pay for living. It is the very purpose of life and not something you do in your spare time" (quoted in National PTA, 2000, p. 87). Unfortunately, a number of barriers prevent many citizens from volunteering in schools. Busy schedules are an

Form 5.1   True or False

TRUE OR FALSE?

___ Successful volunteer recruitment is measured by the number of volunteers.

___ Potential volunteers should never be denied the right to volunteer.

___ Volunteers who have experience working with children do not require training.

___ Volunteers do not need regular feedback about their performance.

___ If performance feedback is given, "negative feedback" should be avoided.

___ Volunteers cannot be fired.

___ One person should be designated with sole responsibility for volunteer recognition.

---

obvious constraint, but this is not insurmountable if people have a genuine interest in volunteering. The school has a responsibility to take the first step and invite citizens to volunteer, rather than waiting for people to come forward. Care must be taken to assign volunteers to tasks that are personally meaningful and rewarding. Volunteers can quickly be "turned off" if they are asked to do something they have no interest in or if they feel they lack the necessary competence to do a job well. Volunteers also express frustration if they are not adequately prepared to handle discipline issues.

Here's a quick true/false quiz (see Form 5.1) to test your knowledge of what it takes to manage a successful volunteer program.

The correct answer to each question is "False." In many ways, managing a successful volunteer program is similar to managing paid employees. The volunteer management plan starts by assessing the need for volunteers and soliciting input from administrators, teachers, and support staff. It is best if educators can be flexible and consider work that volunteers can do at home as well as at school. Job descriptions can be created for regular volunteers, much like they would be for paid employees. Creativity can pay big dividends at the recruitment stage. To attract senior volunteers, some schools have hosted open houses at local senior centers or churches. To encourage parent volunteers, schools can work with local employers to include tips on parent involvement in employee paychecks (National PTA, 2000). Potential volunteers should then be carefully screened for interests, skills, and any possible issues that might compromise the safety of children. Depending on district policy, a criminal background check may or may not be necessary unless the adult will be working alone with an individual child, but reference checks are a good idea for those who will be volunteering on a regular basis. It may be necessary to turn away a prospective volunteer who does not appear to be well suited to work with children.

Once a new volunteer arrives at school, some degree of orientation and training is appropriate, just as it would be for a new employee. The new volunteer will need to become acquainted with the school facilities, as well as with its policies and procedures. It is critically important that the volunteer has meaningful work waiting for him or her; scrambling to find work for the volunteer sends the message that his or her time is not appreciated. When assigning volunteers to various tasks, it helps to consider the volunteer's motivation for volunteering. The reasons for volunteering are varied. Some people volunteer to gain experience, others may want to meet new people, while someone else may have purely altruistic motives. For example, a volunteer with a high need to socialize will be unhappy if he or she is alone in the copy room for long periods of time, making it harder to retain this volunteer.

Feedback and recognition are also important in retaining volunteers. Volunteers need regular feedback on their performance, as would paid employees. This includes feedback on areas needing improvement, as well as recognition of success. In some cases, it may be necessary to terminate the relationship with a volunteer if no other options exist. Successful volunteers need to feel appreciated in a way that is personally appropriate. Formal, public recognition may be more important for some, while others may prefer more private and personal gestures. Recognition is most effective when it is a joint effort; in other words, the volunteer's contribution is appreciated by more than one person. It is everyone's responsibility to make the volunteer feel welcome and appreciated.

Volunteer opportunities are a great way to engage parents and other members of the community in the life of the school. At Berkman Elementary School in Round Rock, Texas, teachers, students, parents, and members of the business community have worked together to create "Excel City," a student-run model city that has its own businesses, government, and monetary systems (National PTA, 2000). Excel City has a bank, a post office, a newspaper, and a variety of stores. Students earn play money to spend at these stores through good conduct, regular attendance, and academic achievement. Fifth graders have the added responsibility of serving as employers and elected officials. Almost all of the materials and equipment for Excel City are donated by parents and community members. Parents are also involved in training students for their roles in Excel City, overseeing student elections, chaperoning field trips to Round Rock businesses, and assisting with fundraising activities. In countless other schools across the country, parents, seniors, and employees from local organizations can be found spending time with children. Partnerships between schools and local employers can be an especially effective way to engage members of the community who otherwise would have minimal contact with public schools.

Partnerships with Community Organizations

The Washington Community School in Indianapolis, Indiana, benefits from partnerships with nearby businesses, public agencies (health care, law enforcement, parks and recreation), and more than 34 nonprofit organizations (including Big Sisters, community centers, and local universities)

(Coalition for Community Schools, 2002). Their joint efforts have helped the school increase the number of students who meet the state standards in language arts and mathematics. Along the way, relationships have been built at personal and institutional levels, raising the level of awareness and understanding of public schools and engaging a broad cross-section of the community. This section will provide a sampling of successful school-community partnerships to illustrate the creativity and variety that characterizes these relationships.

The local business community typically provides a number of partnership opportunities. "Adopt-a-school" programs are popular, where a local business may provide volunteers and donations of furniture, computers, and other equipment. Verizon, The Federal Reserve Bank of Boston, and Gillette are working with Dorchester and Boston high schools to improve the test scores of their summer student employees through a "Classroom at the Workplace" program (Partnership for Family Involvement in Education, 2002). Target Stores have launched a "Take Charge of Education Program" to provide funds to schools through grants, scholarships, and donations. Recently, Target joined forces with the U.S. Department of Education to support the "No Child Left Behind" initiative. Through Target's "Lullaby Club" baby registry kiosks, they will be able to reach more than 500,000 expectant parents with messages about the importance of reading to children. Larger businesses certainly have their advantages as potential partners, but smaller businesses should not be overlooked. A local pizza restaurant can donate pizza to classrooms as incentives for student achievement, or the local beauty salon can provide hair stylists to the school so that low-income children can receive much needed haircuts. Employers of any size can facilitate engaged parenting by offering flextime, part-time work options, telecommuting, and time off for school activities. Some companies even offer classes in parenting.

Libraries also make great partners for schools. A school could work with the local library and bookstores to host a book fair. Some of the activities might include storytelling, puppet shows, and used-book exchanges (National PTA, 2000). This is also a perfect opportunity to make sure families have library cards. In DeForest, Wisconsin, the school district and the local public library jointly sponsor a family involvement and literacy program (Funkhouser et al., 1997). They offer early childhood education, parenting education, and adult education programs, as well as career exploration workshops for high school students. The program also produces and distributes self-contained family activity kits each week to all Title I families in the district. (Title I of the federal Elementary and Secondary Education Act of 1965 is intended to improve the academic achievement of the disadvantaged student.) In support of the local schools, the library circulates copies of the district curriculum and objectives as well as videotapes of school events, such as concerts and plays. These are greatly appreciated by those who are unable to attend the performances.

As partners with schools, health care agencies can provide much needed medical and dental services to low-income students. In some communities, the health care professionals travel to the schools to deliver the services. The East Elementary School in rural North Carolina partnered with the county health department to open a satellite health clinic near the school (Coalition for Community Schools, 2002). The clinic provides immunizations and treatment for conditions requiring immediate attention, such as head lice. Other schools host an annual health fair in partnership with community healthcare providers (National PTA, 2000). Booths inform parents and students about a variety of health topics and possible careers in health care. Paramedics can be invited to demonstrate emergency medical care or safety techniques.

Partnerships with higher education can also be quite valuable to public schools. "Teach Baltimore," based at Johns Hopkins University, works with public schools across the city to reduce summer learning loss among students (Partnership for Family Involvement in Education, 2002). Baldwin-Wallace College in Cleveland, Ohio, provides parents with classes in parent-child communication, while Temple University in Philadelphia trains teachers on how to increase parent involvement (Funkhouser et al., 1997). Thomas Gardner Extended Services School in Boston reaps many rewards from its partnership with Boston College. Graduate and undergraduate students, as well as faculty, work at the school daily. A Parents Center, staffed by Boston College law students, hosts weekly coffees and work shops on issues like immigration (Coalition for Community Schools, 2000).

The possibilities for school-community partnerships are endless. Arts organizations can provide professional development opportunities for teachers and experiential learning opportunities for children. Media organizations can offer expertise in communication training and in the use of newspapers as a teaching tool. And partnerships with social service agencies offer benefits too numerous to mention. Most school districts will probably have some partnerships already in place. The key is to manage these partnerships for maximum impact. The following checklist (adapted from Blank & Langford, 2000) can be useful in evaluating existing partnerships:

- Do we have clearly identified goals for this partnership?
- Are there well-defined roles for each partner to play?
- Is there regular, effective communication between partners?
- Is there smooth coordination of activities?
- Are we doing a good job of promoting our successes?
- Are we making efforts to expand the base of involvement via this partnership?
- How would we evaluate the current and potential value of this partnership? What is working? What isn't?

Thus, a partnership between a school and a community organization requires the same types of skills needed in managing any relationship: clear purpose, good communication, and coordinated efforts. Evaluation is important as well, in order to identify areas for improvement and to look for opportunities to leverage this relationship for greater impact. Jehl et al. (2001) propose a five-step process of engagement for community building that serves as a great synthesis of key ideas from the current and previous chapters:

1. *Find out* about constituent interests and needs.

2. *Reach out* to potential partners.

3. *Spell out* the purpose and the terms of the partnership.

4. *Work out* difficulties as they arise, making necessary modifications.

5. *Build out* from success by using it to leverage expanded efforts.

So far, this chapter has presented numerous strategies for making connections with parents and community members, encouraging them to become more involved in the life of the public school. The time they spend in various activities that support student learning has a direct positive impact on student achievement. This involvement is also very likely to make parents and community members more sensitive to the funding challenges facing most school districts. This will pay dividends if it becomes necessary to raise taxes to support public schools. A detailed discussion of strategies for passing bond issues and levy referenda is beyond the scope of this book, but the National School Public Relations Association has some excellent resources on this topic (*www.nspra.org*).

To keep parents and community members involved in the life of public schools over the longer term, it would seem appropriate to provide them permanent representation in the decision-making process to determine goals and priorities for public schools. Issues to be addressed might include creating standards for student achievement, strategies for increasing school funding, and programs for improving student achievement, among others. Until recently, opportunities for community members to become involved in school policy decisions have been limited. Citizens could perhaps run for a school board position or mobilize others to lobby board members and school administrators. The advent of school-based management has provided community members with an expanded opportunity to participate in educational policy decision making.

School-Based Management

Site councils, or school-based management systems, delegate authority for managing a school to those who work in the school, parents of current students in that school, or taxpaying community members within that school's geographic boundaries. This is in contrast to a more traditional decision-making model confined to administrators at the district and building level. Most of the successful community engagement initiatives described in Chapter Two use school-based management systems. The decentralized decision making that characterizes school-based management has a number of important advantages (Mauriel & Jenni, 1989). These include the following:

- Better decisions that account for the unique needs of an individual school and that consider diverse perspectives of educators and community members. These decisions should ultimately result in improved student achievement.
- More timely decisions instead of relying on already overburdened administrators
- Greater ownership and support of decisions at the school level
- Potential for better cost control and more specific accountability because responsibility is assigned at the school level rather than at the district level

I have personally observed the power of school-based management while serving on the site council of my children's elementary school. We were facing a budget crunch, and it was time to develop a staffing plan for the coming school year. The certified teachers on the site council were reluctant to substitute paraprofessionals for certified teachers in order to make the dollars go further. They certainly had legitimate concerns about the future of their profession if this practice were to become commonplace. Parents came into the discussion wanting lower student-to-adult ratios in the classroom, with little concern for whether the adult was a certified teacher or a paraprofessional. The ensuing discussion allowed teachers and parents to hear and understand each other's concerns. As a result, we were able to craft a compromise plan that had unanimous support rather than taking an approach that left one group feeling as if they had lost.

There are also drawbacks associated with the use of site councils, however. The process of group decision making can be more time consuming than a decision made by a single individual. Another common complaint is that parents and community members lack the professional background in education, thereby limiting their decision-making capabilities. Confidentiality may be a concern if personnel decisions need to be made regarding a specific employee. And building principals may find it difficult to be held ultimately accountable for a decision over which they had only partial control. School-based management systems have received mixed reviews, due, in part, to the fact that responsibility for decision making has not always been accompanied by the necessary authority and resources to implement decisions. In order to reap the benefits of a successful school-based management system, careful attention must be paid to defining responsibilities, accompanied by the necessary authority and resources to address these responsibilities. Guidelines for site-council structure and process also need to be specified.

Responsibilities, Authority, and Resources

One of the first issues to be addressed is the scope of the site council's decision-making responsibilities. Which types of decisions are most appropriately made at the central district office and which decisions should be made at the building level? For those decisions to be made at the building level, which should be made by the principal alone and which should be within the domain of the site council? Each school district will need to determine how these responsibilities are to be assigned. Districts will vary in the degree to which they delegate decision-making responsibility to site councils. It is critically important, however, that these responsibilities be clearly understood by all parties involved; otherwise, confusion and frustration will result. In addition, the National School Boards Association advises that schools be granted discretion over budgets, staffing, and program design related to those responsibilities. Individual schools also need access to information from the district in accordance with these responsibilities (Drury, 1999). Failure to provide authority, information, and control over resources will hamper the efforts of schools to assume more decision-making responsibility. Table 5.2 provides a summary of key decision areas to be addressed in assigning responsibilities.

Site Council Structure

Another important consideration to be addressed when implementing school-based management is the size of the site council and representation on the council. The ideal size for a decision-making group has been debated for years; the challenge is to balance the need for varied perspectives with decision-making efficiency. Groups larger than 15 members do tend to fractionate, and individual members feel less responsible for decision outcomes. Small groups (fewer than five to seven members) may be limited in the variety of ideas and perspectives represented. Each school will need to determine the council size that is most practical for the situation. It *is* a good idea to have an even number of members, so that school staff and parents/community members can have equal representation. The principal should always be a member of the site council, and teachers should comprise the majority

Table 5.2   Decision-Making Responsibilities

Directions: For each of the following decision areas, place a "B/A" in the blank if this is the primary responsibility of the school board/ district administration. Place an "SC" in the blank if this is the primary responsibility of the site council. Place a "P" in the blank if this is the primary responsibility of the building principal.

___ Adoption of curriculum
___ Designation of desired student outcomes
___ Approval of the budget and allocation of budget to school sites
___ Approval of staffing and allocation of FTE/hours to site
___ Use of staffing equivalencies/ staffing hours
___ Distribution of site budgets
___ Management of the athletics program
___ Policy implementation
___ Contractual/legal personnel issues
___ Curriculum implementation
___ Development of district policy
___ School calendar
___ Transportation system
___ Facilities maintenance program
___ Building material adoption
___ Standardized testing program
___ Building operational procedures
___ Adoption/purchase of major materials for approved curriculum areas
___ Food service
___ Staff development
___ Special education policy, rules, and regulations
___ Development of site mission and goals
___ Principals' job description, evaluation, and appointment
___ Program evaluation

of school staff representatives. Noncertified staff should be represented as well.

In our site council, we had 12 members, 6 of whom were school employees. These included the principal, three to four teachers, and one to two noncertified staff members. All staff positions, except the principal, were elected. The six parent/community positions were also elected, one of whom was required to be a member of the school PTSA as well. This provides for more effective communication between the PTSA and the site council. Parents and school staff need to know whom they may contact if they have an issue to bring before the site council. Members served staggered two-year terms, so that only half of the council turned over each year. We decided that a cochair model of leadership would be most effective in representing the concerns of school staff and parent/community members, but, in any case, a chair or chairs need to be selected along with a secretary to keep minutes.

Process Issues

The scheduling of a "convenient" meeting time for both parents and school staff can prove to be challenging. School staff prefer to meet immediately following the end of the school day. Parents and community members tend to prefer early morning or evening meetings to avoid conflicts with work schedules. Our site council alternated monthly meeting times; we met at 3:00 P.M. one month and at 7:00 P.M. the following month. Meeting dates and times were set at the beginning of the school year and were publicized in advance. Each meeting had a printed agenda and was conducted using standard rules of parliamentary procedure.

Another important process consideration is the issue of voting. What will constitute a necessary quorum in order to conduct business? Will consensus decision making be the goal, or will voting be used to make decisions? If voting is used, what will constitute a majority? Will absentee ballots be allowed? If these issues can be addressed and summarized in a statement of bylaws, this will reduce confusion and controversy regarding subsequent decisions.

The effectiveness of school-based management depends on clear guidelines for site council structure and the process to be used in decision making. Site councils need to understand which decisions are within the scope of their responsibility and which decisions will be made by teachers, administrators, or board members. And site councils need access to information and financial resources, in addition to the necessary authority for decision making. The school board and district administration have the responsibility to create an infrastructure for school-based management that addresses all of these issues.

KEEPING THE COMMUNITY ENGAGED

A variety of strategies may be useful to educators as they engage their communities in the work of public schools. But each community will need to develop its own plan for sustaining the momentum generated by the community engagement process. How will citizens be involved in the action plans they helped to shape? How will schools keep citizens informed on the progress toward common goals? What new structures or processes are needed to support shared responsibility in decision making and subsequent action? Who will coordinate these activities? Can these responsibilities be accommodated within existing positions or do new positions need to be added as financial resources permit? Community engagement represents a paradigm shift in the way we think about the relationship between public schools and their communities. How can we better prepare educators and citizens for this collaborative relationship? That is the topic to be addressed in the next chapter.

DISCUSSION QUESTIONS FOR CHAPTER 5

1. For each of the constituent groups (and subgroups when appropriate) identified in Table 3.1 (see page 46):
   a. Are there key contact persons within these constituent groups or subgroups?

  b. Who are the district employees with connections to each of these constituent groups or contact persons?
  c. What type of involvement from this constituent group would we like to encourage? (More than one type of involvement is possible.)
  - Family support of student learning at home and school
  - Volunteerism
  - Partnerships with community organizations
  - Ongoing involvement in school/district policy decisions
  - Support for funding initiatives

  d. What is necessary to make this type of involvement a reality?

2. Prioritize planned efforts to engage constituent groups as identified in question 1.

3. If parents and community members are to play a greater role in school decision-making processes, for which types of decisions should they:
  - Serve on the decision-making body?
  - Serve in an advisory capacity?
  - Defer to decisions made by board members and administrators?

4. What impact will continuing engagement efforts have on existing structure and processes at the school or district level? Will resources and/or responsibilities need to be reassigned? Will district employees assume all or part of the ongoing responsibility for these efforts?

Sustaining
the Community
Engagement Process

In the immediate future, significant effort will be necessary in order to "put the 'public' back in public schools." The work will be time consuming, often difficult, and perhaps awkward at first. Community engagement differs from more traditional models of interaction between schools and the public they serve. Educators need training in what is meant by "community engagement" and the methods used to make it happen. At the same time, the public needs to "step up to the plate" in terms of their level of involvement in public institutions. Certainly parents can be trained in how to become more involved in their child's school, but the task of engaging the community as a whole presents a greater challenge. For adults, habits of apathy and self-interest are hard to overcome. The most effective strategy may be to target today's youth with clearer expectations and greater guidance regarding the responsibilities of citizenship in a democratic society.

TRAINING FOR EDUCATORS

Resources for training educators in the techniques of community engagement have grown in number in recent years, but there is room for improvement. Most of the professional development opportunities related to community engagement focus on the issue of parent involvement. The National PTA (2000) has developed a set of National Standards for Parent/Family Involvement Programs, using Epstein's (1995) six types of school-family-community involvement that were discussed in Chapter Five. These standards can be used by schools as an assessment tool to identify areas needing improvement and also as a source of "best practice" ideas. It is critically important to give all educators a voice in the design of their own professional development programs. This will give individual educators ownership in their own development and ensure that the skills acquired will be relevant to their daily responsibilities. Darling-Hammond and McLaughlin (1995) have summarized several key characteristics of all successful professional development programs:

- They must engage teachers in concrete tasks of teaching, assessment, observation, and reflection.
- They must be participant driven.
- They must ultimately be connected to teachers' work with students.
- They must be collaborative, focusing on a sharing of knowledge in the educator's community of practice.
- They must be sustained, ongoing, and focused on collective efforts to solve problems of practice.
- They must be connected to other aspects of school change.

Once the professional development needs have been identified, local colleges and universities may offer specific training on how to encourage parent involvement, as is the case at Temple University in Philadelphia (Funkhouser, Gonzales, & Moles, 1997). The Institute for Responsive Education at Northeastern University and the Center on

School, Family, and Community Partnerships at Johns Hopkins University also provide information and training resources on parent involvement strategies. (See the listing of Internet sources following this chapter.) Some programs bring parents and educators together for training in involvement strategies. Camp Kieve, a leadership training institute that serves the northeastern United States and Canada, offers retreats for parents and teachers that focus on increasing parent and community involvement (Funkhouser et al., 1997). Appendix D of the Funkhouser et al. report on family involvement provides a listing of resources for building successful school/family partnerships. It can be found at: *http://www.ed.gov/pubs/FamInvolve*.

Educators may also be interested in training opportunities and support materials related to the use of some of the specific engagement techniques addressed in earlier chapters. Where can we learn to plan and facilitate a large-group event like a town meeting or a Future Search conference? Where can we obtain materials on the use of study circles or the Community Conversation kit used by the Harwood Institute? Where can we find materials to help educators to do a better job of listening to and interpreting community concerns without professional bias? Contact information for these and other resources can be found in the listing of Internet sources that follows this chapter.

In reality, professional development programs can only go so far in preparing educators for the practice of community engagement. Professional development funds are limited, and the shortage of substitute teachers in many districts further restricts this type of activity. Ideally, community engagement strategies should be embedded within the curriculum used in teacher and administrator education programs. If it is not feasible to offer separate courses in community engagement, then these concepts should be included within existing courses. Educators should be asked to demonstrate a minimum acceptable level of competency in using community engagement strategies as part of the requirements for licensure.

At present, only the topic of parent involvement is being addressed in education curricula, and then typically only in early childhood or special education courses. No state requires course work in parent involvement or community engagement in general for licensure, recertification, or renewal of a license (National PTA, 2002). However, the National Council for Accreditation of Teacher Education (NCATE) and the National Association of State Directors of Teacher Education and Certification (NASDTEC) have both recently added or strengthened standards related specifically to parent involvement. And the National Board for Professional Teacher Standards has also addressed parent involvement in its standards. This progress is encouraging, but more work is needed to guarantee that all educators have some level of skill in engaging the public as part of their education curriculum and their licensure requirement.

TRAINING FOR PARENTS AND COMMUNITY MEMBERS

Fewer opportunities are available for training parents and community members in how to become more involved in their public schools and other public institutions. This may be due to the fact that previous generations had a greater sense of civic responsibility, making these types of programs unnecessary. As Putnam (2000) and others have documented, the post–World War II generations have been less engaged with public institutions. It is not fair to place sole responsibility for motivating community involvement on the shoulders of educators. The community has an obligation to come forward, assuming they understand the duties of citizenship, in general, and parenthood, in particular. But what if the community does not understand the responsibilities of citizenship and/or parenthood? What if they lack an understanding of how to execute those responsibilities?

Fortunately, training programs for parents on how to become more involved in their child's education are quite numerous. A model program is the Commonwealth Institute for Parent Leadership in Kentucky (CIPL). CIPL is "designed to make parents more powerful as they become effective advocates for improved education and higher achievement for all students. The Institute seeks to create a new level of parent engagement in the state, and it reaches all parents-including those who have the most difficulty being involved" (About CIPL, para. 6). Two hundred participants are chosen each year from throughout the state of Kentucky to take part in three two-day sessions. The curriculum of these sessions addresses the interpretation of academic achievement data, leadership training, group process skills, and how to organize for action.

Not every parent is interested in becoming a more effective advocate for school reform and improving student achievement for all students, however. Some parents lack the basic information needed to support their own child in school. Many school districts offer training in how to help with homework, college planning, and the use of computer technology. Some districts open their professional development opportunities to interested parents, when appropriate. For example, if an inservice program is dealing with strategies for teaching special-needs students or gifted students, parents may also be invited. Community education programs offer numerous courses in basic parenting skills. Local colleges and universities may offer occasional programs on topics of interest to parents, such as how to more effectively communicate with an adolescent child. The challenge is not to merely increase the number of programs available to parents, but also to make sure that these programs are addressing the needs of parents and that they are made available to the parents who most need them.

Unlike parent education, training programs in citizenship are fewer in number. Some communities do offer programs in citizen involvement and leadership. In Santa Barbara, California, for example, the Center for Community Education and Citizen Participation (Cirone & Margerum, 1987) was designed to provide "hands-on, community-based literacy programs for adults" (p. 218). In Minnesota, the Citizens League is a nonprofit organization that promotes the public interest by involving citizens in identifying and framing critical public policy choices, making recommendations, and advocating for their implementation. The problem with these programs is not their content but their limited reach. Only a handful of citizens will have the motivation and the opportunity to participate in one of these programs. By the time most of us reach adulthood, we have already developed bad habits unless we are taught otherwise. The best opportunity for teaching citizenship occurs in our youth so that we learn to get into the habit of being involved at an early age. And institutions like schools have the potential to reach a large proportion of the population with these important lessons.

TRAINING FOR YOUTH

In Chapter One, we saw that the concept of social capital is critical to community engagement. Putnam (2000) described social capital as "connections among individuals—social networks and the norms of reciprocity and trustworthiness that arise from them" (p. 19). These connections bring an awareness of a greater good outside of one's own self-interest, providing the motivation to engage and become involved. Housed in the Kennedy School of Government at Harvard University, the Saguaro Seminar on Civic Engagement in America (2000) has addressed the issue of youth and social capital. Research from the Saguaro Seminar suggests that three institutions play a major role in the formation of social capital in young people between the ages of 10 and 21: schools, community organizations, and families. For each of these three institutions, the Saguaro Seminar offers the following recommendations for building social capital:

SCHOOLS:

Require community service of all students

Create smaller schools

Restore extracurricular activities

Make "civics" relevant to young people

Reconnect and reengage school dropouts

COMMUNITY ORGANIZATIONS:

Foster intergenerational mentoring

Support the community service movement

Put young people on community boards and councils

Recognize the capacity of adolescents and the circumstances that support their contributions

Make contributions count by providing access to scholarships or jobs

Recognize those who support youth involvement

Strengthen intermediaries between schools and community organizations

FAMILIES:

Revive "family time"

Different communities have taken different approaches to developing citizenship skills in young people. The Campaign for Fiscal Equity sponsors an annual conference every May titled "Model Society: My School, My Community, My Rights." Offered to students in the state of New York, the conference allows students to become part of a simulated model community where they face voter apathy, community isolation, and underfunding of schools. The students then have the opportunity to make policy decisions to address the most pressing issues facing the community (Model Society, 2002, para. 2). In Spokane, Washington, the Chase Youth Commission was founded in 1985 to foster youth involvement, leadership, recognition, and empowerment (Benham & Ouellette, 2002). Reinforcing many of the recommendations made by the Saguaro Seminar, the Chase Youth Commission offers annual awards to youth who demonstrate excellence in the following categories: citizenship, community service, leadership, creativity, diversity, courage, and personal achievement. The Chase Youth Commission also provides a forum for Spokane youth to ask questions of candidates for local office and provides opportunities for youth participation in city and county advisory boards, commissions, and committees.

Schools themselves may be the key to ensuring that future generations understand the responsibilities of citizenship and are motivated to act in fulfilling those responsibilities for the benefit of schools and other public institutions. Community service is a basic requirement for graduation from high school in many states. Educators are exploring new ways to teach citizenship as part of the standard curriculum at all grade levels.

Higher education can also play a role in preparing citizens of the future. Rutgers University is one of a number of colleges and universities that have experimented with programs to teach citizenship, including classroom civic education and community service requirements (Barber, 1992). Paul Rogat Loeb (1999) makes a compelling argument for teaching college students how to become active participants in a democracy. How does one go about advocating for change in our society? Does becoming an "activist" require extremist views and violent behavior, or are there other strategies of activism? College professors are currently very effective in presenting the complexity of the challenges facing American society, but they are not as diligent in addressing the strategies that individual citizens might use to address these challenges. As a result, students often come away from these discussions feeling overwhelmed and powerless. All of us can learn from the stories of successful change agents, whether these agents live in our neighborhoods today or in times past. We can learn not only what these activists were able to accomplish but, more important, *how* they did it. This can provide each one of us with the tools as well as the inspiration to build more engaged communities.

A Brighter Future for Public Schools

As Loeb (1999) builds his case for teaching activism, he is quick to point out that hope is necessary in order for an individual to take action. Hopelessness and cynicism are pervasive in American society today. We need to believe that our contribution can make a difference in order to take that first step. Educators will need to provide a vision of a brighter future for public schools as they work to engage their communities. How would public schools be different in a community that is fully engaged in the education of its youth? What resources would be available to students? What would individual students be able to achieve? How would the community, as a whole, benefit from these strong and successful schools? The next logical question is then "How do we get there?"

What actions are necessary to make our vision of the future a reality? For parents, it may mean greater involvement in the education of their children. For businesses and other institutions within the community, it may mean more effective partnerships with public schools. For other citizens, it may mean volunteering in the public schools or supporting funding initiatives. Over time, as commitment and conviction deepen, citizens will be in a position to advocate at the local, state, and federal levels for the policy changes necessary to ensure that each child has the opportunity to achieve his or her full potential. If schools are "the public nurseries of our future" (Barber, 1992, p. 263), the result will be a brighter future for all of us.

DISCUSSION QUESTIONS FOR CHAPTER 6

1. What are our school/district's professional development needs for:
   a. Use of techniques to understand constituent perceptions?
   b. Design and implementation of strategies to further engage targeted constituent groups (i.e., parent involvement)?
   c. Maintenance and evaluation of an ongoing community engagement process?

2. What can we do to educate or remind citizens that they share responsibility with the public schools for educating the community's youth? How do we provide citizens with a vision of a better future for public schools?

3. What can we do to better prepare our youth for the responsibilities of citizenship?

Resource

Summary of Internet Sources

WHERE CAN I FIND INFORMATION ON PARENT INVOLVEMENT STRATEGIES?

For ideas to encourage family involvement in public schools and a listing of resources: *www.ed.gov/pubs/FamInvolve*

For information on the National Standards for Parent/Family Involvement Programs: *www.pta.org/parentinvolvement/standards/index.asp*

For links and publications through the National Coalition for Parent Involvement in Education: *www.ncpie.org*

For training opportunities and publications from the Institute for Responsive Education at Northeastern University: *www.responsiveeducation.org*

For information and a list of publications from the Center on School, Family, and Community Partnerships at Johns Hopkins University: *www.csos.jhu.edu/p2000/center.htm*

For training resources from Parent Leadership Associates to develop parent leaders: www.plassociates.org.

What Is a "Community School"?

For information on the concept of community schools: *www.communityschools.org*

What Techniques Are Available for Understanding and Engaging Constituents?

For publications from Public Education Network, addressing tools and techniques for community engagement, including the use of local education funds: *www.publiceducation.org*

For information on roundtable discussions and other materials from the Campaign for Fiscal Equity, Inc: *www.cfequity.org*

For tools related to the "Reconnecting Communities and Schools" initiative from the Harwood Institute: *www.theharwoodinstitute.org/initiatives/reconnecting.shtml*

For materials on the use of study circles through Study Circles Resource Center: *www.studycircles.org*

For National Issues Forums discussion guides: www.publicagenda.org/aboutpa/aboutpa4.htm.

For courses on planning and facilitating large-group events offered by the International Association for Public Participation: *www.iap2.org*

For training and information on the use of Future Search Conferences: *www.futuresearch.net*

References

About CIPL. Retrieved July 18, 2002, from *www.cipl.org/about.html*

Alreck, P. L., and Settle, R.B. (1994). *The Survey Research Handbook.* (2d ed.). New York: McGraw-Hill/Irwin.

Annenberg Institute for School Reform. (1998). *Reasons for Hope, Voices for Change.* Providence, RI: Brown University Press.

Armistead, L. (1999). Professional PR Functions: News Media Relations. In K. Muir (Ed.), *School Public Relations: Building Confidence in Education* (pp. 67–82). Rockville, MD: National School Public Relations Association.

Barber, B. R. (1992). *An Aristocracy of Everyone: The Politics of Education and the Future of America.* New York: Oxford University Press.

Benham, J., and Ouellette, M. (2002, July 1). Spokane Focuses on Youth. Retrieved July 18, 2002, from *www.nlc.org/nlc_org/site/newsroom/*

Blank, M. J., & Langford, B. H. (2000). *Strengthening Partnerships: Community School Assessment Checklist.* Coalition for Community Schools. Retrieved August 1, 2002, from *www.communityschools. org/assessmentnew.pdf*

Bunker, B. B., & Alban, B. T. (1997). *Large Group Intervention: Engaging the Whole System for Rapid Change.* San Francisco: Jossey-Bass.

Campaign for Fiscal Equity, Inc (CFE). (2000, October). *In Evidence: Policy Reports from the CFE Trial, Setting the Standard for a Sound Basic Education.* Volume 1. Retrieved July 18, 2002, from *www.cfe-quity. org/standards.pdf*

Charlotte-Mecklenburg Education Foundation. (2002). *State of Public Education Report, Destination: Excellence.* Retrieved July 18, 2002, from *www.advocatesfored.org/publications/CMEF%20SOPER% 202002.pdf*

Cirone, W. J., & Margerum, B. (1987, May–June). Models of Citizen Involvement and Community Education. *National Civic Review,* 76 (3), 217–223.

The Coalition for Community Schools. (2000). *Community Schools: Partnerships for Excellence.* Washington, DC: Institute for Educational

Leadership. Retrieved August 1, 2002, from *www.communityschools. org/pubs.coal.html*

The Coalition for Community Schools. (2002). *A Handbook for State Policy Leaders: Community Schools.* Washington, DC: Institute for Educational Leadership. Retrieved August 1, 2002, from *www.communityschools.org/pubs.coal.html*

Cox, J. (1996). *Your Opinion, Please! How to Build the Best Questionnaires in the Field of Education.* Thousand Oaks, CA: Corwin Press.

Cuban, L. (2000). Why Is it So Hard to Get 'Good' Schools? In L. Cuban and D. Shipps (Eds.), *Reconstructing the Common Good in Education* (pp. 148–69). Stanford, CA: Stanford University Press.

Danzberger, J. P., & Friedman, W. (1997, June). Public Conversations about the Public's Schools. *Phi Delta Kappan, 78* (10), 744–748.

Darling-Hammond, L., & McLaughlin, M. W. (1995, April). Policies that Support Professional Development in an Era of Reform. *Phi Delta Kappan, 76* (8), 597–604.

Decker, L. E. (2001, September). Allies in Education. *Principal Leadership, 2* (1), 42–46.

Drury, D. W. (1999). *Reinventing School-Based Management: A School Board Guide to School-Based Improvement.* Alexandria, VA: National School Boards Association.

Epstein, J. L. (1995, May). School/Family/Community Partnerships: Caring for the Children We Share. *Phi Delta Kappan, 76* (9), 701–712.

Epstein, J. L., et al. (2002). *School, Family, and Community Partnerships: Your Handbook for Action* (2d ed.).Thousand Oaks, CA: Corwin Press.

Farkas, S., Foley, P., & Duffett, A. (2001). *Just Waiting to be Asked: A Fresh Look at Attitudes on Public Engagement.* New York: Public Agenda.

Fullan, M. (2000). Leadership for the Twenty-First Century: Breaking the Bonds of Dependency. In *The Jossey-Bass Reader on Educational Leadership* (pp. 156–163). San Francisco: Jossey-Bass.

Funkhouser, J. E., Gonzales, M. R., & Moles, O. C. (1997). *Family Involvement in Children's Education: Successful Local Approaches.* Washington, DC: U.S. Department of Education, Office of Educational Research and Improvement. Retrieved August 1, 2002, from *www.ed.gov/pubs/FamInvolve*

Glickman, C. D. (1993). *Renewing America's Schools: A Guide for School-Based Action.* San Francisco: Jossey-Bass.

Goodlad, J. I. (1994). *What Schools Are For* (2d ed.). Bloomington, IN: Phi Delta Kappa Educational Foundation.

Harwood, R. C. (2001). Public Benefit: Entrée or Side Dish? *The Nonprofit Quarterly, 2,* 16–19.

The Harwood Institute. (2000a). *Community Conversation Kit.* Bethesda, MD: author.

The Harwood Institute. (2000b). *Generating a New Public Story.* Bethesda, MD: author.

The Harwood Institute. (2000c). *Professionalism Barometer.* Bethesda, MD: author.

Henderson, A. T., & Berla, N. (Eds.) (1994). *A New Generation of Evidence: The Family Is Critical to Student Achievement.* Washington, DC: Center for Law and Education.

Henderson, A. T., & Mapp, K. L. (2002). *A New Wave of Evidence: The Impact of School, Family, and Community Connections on Student Achievement.* Austin, TX: The National Center for Family and Community Connections with Schools. Retrieved April 8, 2003, from *www.sedl.org/connections*

Henderson, A. T., & Raimondo, B. (2002, February). Every Child Counts: Citizens Tackle School District's Achievement Gap. *Middle Ground, 5*(4). Retrieved July 18, 2002, from *www.cipl. org/pubs/every_child_article.pdf*

Himmelman, A. T. (1994). Communities Working Collaboratively for Change. In M. Herman (Ed.), *Resolving Conflict: Strategies for Local Government.* Washington, DC: International City/County Management Association.

Houston, P., & Bryant, A. (1997, June). The Roles of Superintendents and School Boards in Engaging the Public with the Public Schools. *Phi Delta Kappan, 78* (10), 756–759.

Jayanthi, M,. & Nelson, J. S. (2002). *Savvy Decision Making: An Administrator's Guide to Using Focus Groups in Schools.* Thousand Oaks, CA: Corwin Press.

Jefferson County Community Accountability Team. (2001). Every Child Counts: Raising Student Achievement in the Middle Grades. Retrieved July 18, 2002, from *www.cipl.org/pubs/cat/ every_child.*

Jehl, J., Blank, M. J., & McCloud, B. (2001). *Education and Community Building: Connecting Two Worlds.* Washington, DC: Institute for Educational Leadership. Retrieved August 1, 2002, from *www.communityschools.org/pubs.partners.html*

Jennings, J. F. (1997, June). An Experiment in Democracy. *Phi Delta Kappan, 78* (10), 769–771.

Kimpton, J. S., and Considine, J. W. (1999, September). The Tough Sledding of District-Led Engagement. *The School Administrator, 56* (8), 6–10.

Kotter, J. P. (1996). *Leading Change.* Boston, MA: Harvard Business School Press.

Kretzmann, J. P., & McKnight, J. L. (1993). *Building Communities from the Inside Out: A Path Toward Finding and Mobilizing A Community's Assets.* Chicago, IL: ACTA.

Krueger, R. A. (1994). *Focus Groups: A Practical Guide for Applied Research* (2d ed.).Thousand Oaks, CA: Sage.

Leighninger, M., & Niedergang, M. (1995a). *The Busy Citizen's Discussion Guide: Education in Our Communities.* Prepared by the Study Circles Resource Center. Pomfret, CT: Topsfield Foundation.

Leighninger, M., & Niedergang, M. (1995b). *Education: How Can Schools and Communities Work Together to Meet the Challenge?* Prepared by the Study Circles Resource Center. Pomfret, CT: Topsfield Foundation.

Loeb, P. R. (1999). *Soul of a Citizen: Living with Conviction in a Cynical Time.* New York: St. Martin's.

Marty, M. (2001, January 5). E-mail communication to St. Olaf College faculty.

Mathews, D. (1994). *Politics for People.* Urbana: University of Illinois Press.

Mathews, D. (1996). *Is There a Public for Public Schools?* Dayton, OH: Kettering Foundation.

Mauriel, J., & Jenni, R. (1989). *School Based Management: Fallacies and Facts.* (Advanced Management Practices Paper #7). Strategic Management Research Center, University of Minnesota.

McDonnell, L. M., & Weatherford, M. S. (1999, November). *Deliberation Is Not Monolithic: Unpacking the Ideal in the Real World.* Paper presented at the annual research conference of the Association for Public Policy Analysis and Management, Washington, DC.

Meyer, R. H. (1996). Value-Added Indicators of School Performance. In E.A. Hanushek and D.W. Jorgenson (Eds.), *Improving America's Schools: The Role of Incentives* (pp. 197–223). Washington, DC: National Academy Press.

Model Society: My School, My Community, My Rights. Campaign for Fiscal Equity, Inc. Retrieved July 18, 2002, from *www.cfequity.org/modelsociety.html*

National Association of Elementary School Principals. (2001). *Leading Learning Communities: Standards for What Principals Should Know and Be Able to Do.* Created in partnership with Collaborative Communications Group. Alexandria, VA: author.

National Issues Forums. (1999a). *Organizing for Public Deliberation and Moderating a Forum/Study Circle.* Dayton, OH: Kettering Foundation.

National Issues Forums. (1999b). *Public Schools: Is There a Way to Fix Them?* Prepared by Public Agenda. Dubuque, IA: Kendall/Hunt.

National PTA. (2000). *Building Successful Partnerships: A Guide for Developing Parent and Family Involvement Programs.* Bloomington, IN: National Educational Service.

National PTA. (2002). *Challenges and Opportunities.* Retrieved August 1, 2002, from *www.pta.org/parentinvolvement/standards/pfichallenge.asp*

O'Callaghan, W. G., Jr. (Ed.) (1999a). *The Power of Public Engagement: A Beacon of Hope for America's Schools.* Manhattan, KS: The MASTER Teacher.

O'Callaghan, W. G., Jr. (1999b). *Putting the Power of Public Engagement to Work for Your Schools and Community.* Manhattan, KS: The MASTER Teacher.

Partnership for Family Involvement In Education, "Highlights," (2002). Retrieved August 1, 2002, from *http://pfie.ed. gov/newsletter.php3.* The Partnership for Family Involvement In Education is now a regional organization, focusing on the state of Maryland, and can be accessed at *www.thefamilyworks.org*

Public Education Network and Public Agenda. (2000). *Quality Now! Results of National Conversations on Education and Race.* Retrieved August 1, 2002, from *www.publiceducation.org/ pdf/qualitynow.pdf*

Public Education Network. (2001). *Communities at Work: A Guidebook of Strategic Interventions for Community Change.* Retrieved July 18, 2002, from *www.publiceducation.org/ pdf/caw.pdf*

Puriefoy, W. D., & Edwards, V. B. (2002, July). Poll: Who's for Kids and Who's Just Kidding. Retrieved August 1, 2002, from *www.nlc.org/nlc_org/site/newsroom/.* This poll was published as "Accountability for All: What Voters Want from Education Candidates" by Public Education Network and *Education Week;* it can be downloaded from *www.publiceducation.org.*

Putnam, R. D. (2000). *Bowling Alone: The Collapse and Revival of American Community.* New York: Simon & Schuster.

Resnick, M. A. (2000). *Communities Count: A School Board Guide to Public Engagement.* Alexandria, VA: National School Boards Association.

Rolnick, A., & Grunewald, R. (2003). *Early Childhood Development: Economic Development with a High Public Return.* Minneapolis: Federal Reserve Bank working paper.

Rose, L. C., & Gallup, A. M. (2000). *The 32nd Annual Phi Delta Kappa/Gallup Poll of the Public's Attitudes Toward the Public Schools.* Retrieved April 2, 2001, from *www.pdkintl.org/* (see publication archives).

Rose, L. C., & Gallup, A. M. (2002). *The 34th Annual Phi Delta Kappa/Gallup Poll of the Public's Attitudes Toward the Public*

Schools. Retrieved September 28, 2002, from *www.pdkintl.org/ kappan/k0209pol.htm*

Saguaro Seminar on Civic Engagement in America. (2000). *Better Together.* Cambridge: MA: John F. Kennedy School of Government, Harvard University. Retrieved September 20, 2002, from *www.bettertogether.org/report.php3*

Saguaro Seminar on Civic Engagement in America. (2001). *The Social Capital Community Benchmark Survey.* Cambridge, MA: John F. Kennedy School of Government, Harvard University. Retrieved June 7, 2003 from *www.cfsv.org/communitysurvey/results_ pr.html.*

Saks, J. B. (2000). *The Community Connection: Case Studies in Public Engagement.* Alexandria: VA: National School Boards Association.

Sarason, S. B. (1996). *Revisiting the Culture of the School and the Problem of Change.* New York: Teachers College Press.

Sizer, T. R. (1997). The Meanings of "Public Education." In J. I. Goodlad and T.J. McMannon (Eds.), *The Public Purpose of Education and Schooling* (pp. 33-40). San Francisco: Jossey-Bass.

Thomas, S. J. (1999). *Designing Surveys That Work! A Step-by-Step Guide.* Thousand Oaks, CA: Corwin Press.

U. S. Department of Education. (1994). *Strong Families, Strong Schools: Building Community Partnerships for Learning.* Washington, DC: Author.

U.S. Department of Education, Office of the Secretary. (2001). *Back to School, Moving Forward: What* No Child Left Behind *Means for America's Communities.* Retrieved August 1, 2002, from *http://ed. gov/inits/backtoschool/community/part5.html*

Van Slyke, S. (1997, June). Building Community for Public Schools: Challenges and Strategies. *Phi Delta Kappan, 78* (10), 753–755.

Visions of Ground Zero: Voices; Proposals for Downtown Draw Array of Opinions. (2002, July 21). *New York Times,* p. A30.

Wadsworth, D. (1997, June). Building a Strategy for Successful Public Engagement. *Phi Delta Kappan, 78* (10), 749–752.

Ward, J. G. (2000). *Teacher Quality: The Human Resource Factor in Education Reform.* A Critical Issues Paper. Urbana: University of Illinois: Institute of Government and Public Affairs.

Weil, R. (1997, June). The View from Between a Rock and a Hard Place. *Phi Delta Kappan, 78* (10), pp. 760–764.

Weisbord, M. R., & Janoff, S. (1995). *Future Search.* San Francisco: Berrett-Koehler.

Index